CHARLES DARWIN

Makers of Modern Science

CHARLES DARWIN:
Evolution of a Naturalist

Richard Milner

AN INFOBASE HOLDINGS COMPANY

CHARLES DARWIN: Evolution of a Naturalist

Facts On File, Inc.
460 Park Avenue South
New York NY 10016

Library of Congress Cataloging-in-Publication Data
Milner, Richard, 1941–
    Charles Darwin: evolution of a naturalist/Richard Milner.
        p. cm.—(Makers of modern science)
    Includes bibliographical references (p.) and index.
    Summary: Examines the life and work of the renowned biologist who transformed conventional Western thought with his theory of natural selection.
    ISBN 0-8160-2557-6
    1. Darwin, Charles, 1809-1882-—Juvenile literature.
    2. Naturalists—England—Biography—Juvenile literature.
    [1. Darwin, Charles, 1809–1882. 2. Naturalists. 3. Evolution.]
    I. Title. II. Series.
    QH31.D2M55   1993
    575' .0092—dc20   92-37792

A British CIP catalogue record for this book is available from the British Library.

Facts On File books are available at special discounts when purchased in bulk quantities for businesses, associations, institutions or sales promotions. Please call our Special Sales Department in New York at 212/683-2244 or 800/322-8755.

Series interior by Ron Monteleone
Cover design by Catherine Hyman
Composition by Facts On File, Inc./Robert Yaffe
Manufactured by R.R. Donnelley & Sons
Printed in the United States of America

10 9 8 7 6 5 4 3 2 1

This book is printed on acid-free paper.

For Jude Bruno,
with love

Also by Richard Milner

*The Encyclopedia of Evolution: Humanity's Search
for Its Origins*. With a Foreword by
Stephen Jay Gould (New York: Facts On File)

CONTENTS

PHOTO CREDITS

ACKNOWLEDGMENTS

With special thanks to:
Prof. James Moore, for many constructive suggestions
Dr. Ralph Colp, Jr., for helping track down sources
Colleagues and friends at *Natural History Magazine,* especially
Vittorio Maestro, Robert Anderson, Ellen Goldensohn, Lisa Stillman
    Alan Ternes, for giving me a home at the American Museum of
Natural History
    Prof. Donald Stone Sade and *The North Country Naturalist*
Dr. C. Tripp
Mrs. Susan Wilder
Librarians, archivists, and historians at AMNH, especially Nina
Root, Don Jacobson, Joel Sweimler, Sarah Granato, Barbara Mathe,
Carmen Callezo
    Ed Knappman, who instigated this book
James Warren, my patient editor
Dr. Michael and Dr. Barbara MacRoberts
Prof. Stephen Jay Gould
Dr. Malcolm Kottler, Prof. Ernst Mayr
Dr. Henry and Gloria Jarecki
Martin and Kate Cassidy
Melvin Van Peebles
Ivory Milner, Thelma Milner, Judy and Jerry Jennings
Miriam and Ira Wallach Foundation
Dave Bergman, Dr. Eric Korn, the late John Chancellor
    Miss Silverthorne, Bromley Library, England; Colindale News-
paper Library; British Museum Library; New York Public Library;
American Philosophical Society; Darwin Manuscript Library (Bos-
ton and Cambridge, England); Mr. Peter Gautrey; Darwin Museum
(Down House); Mr. Philip Titheradge; Library, Society for Psychic
Research (New York); Mr. Michael Huxley

FOREWORD

by Dr. James A. Moore

Charles Darwin never lost his boyhood fascination with nature. Born in 1809, he grew up on the edge of an English market town, surrounded by woods and wildlife. His mother kept fancy pigeons and his father raised exotic fruit. There were always things to discover, places to explore. Down the hill in his own back yard was the Severn River. Here young Charles was always catching fish or collecting insects and rocks.

Later, as a teenager studying at the University of Edinburgh, Charles dredged up sea creatures and dissected them, eager to see how they reproduced. At Cambridge, where he finished his education, he built up a huge beetle collection and began examining plants. It was then, in 1831, that he received the offer to join the surveying ship HMS *Beagle* on a voyage around the world.

What a wonderful opportunity for a lad "of enlarged curiosity," declared his favorite uncle. In the next five years, Charles made the most of it. Hacking through jungles, clambering up mountains, galloping across arid plains, he proved to himself and his family that he was a top-notch naturalist. His collections were amazing. So were his new ideas—ideas about evolution.

The famous *Beagle* adventure is only the best-known episode in Darwin's lifelong voyage of discovery. In this splendid book, Richard Milner tells the whole story of Darwin's development from boy collector, to *Beagle* naturalist, to Britain's greatest evolutionist. It is a sprightly account, selective but authoritative, suited to young people of all ages.

In the last decade, scholars have pieced together a dazzling new portrait of Darwin from a wealth of untapped materials. Hundreds of his letters were transcribed for the first time, his diary of the *Beagle* voyage freshly edited, and his secret notebooks on evolution published in full. Milner has benefited directly or indirectly from all these sources. His is now the most up-to-date biography of Darwin for young adult readers.

This book also holds treasures that can be found nowhere else. Darwin is known to have served as a county magistrate—a justice of the peace—but Milner gives for the first time precise details of the very cases on which Darwin himself passed judgment. Again, Darwin's antipathy to spiritualism is no secret, but in Chapter 10, Milner reveals the full extent of his campaign against conjuring con artists and their clients, not least his fellow evolutionist Alfred Russel Wallace.

Yet throughout Milner's story, Darwin's dogged curiosity shines through, even when confessing himself to be a "wretched bigot" about spiritualism. A bit of the boy in him never grew old; he never lost his passion to find out nature's secrets. It seems fitting that Darwin ended his life by studying the habits of worms. They had been his companions ever since his childhood fishing trips. In death they always would be.

James A. Moore, Professor of the History of Science at England's Open University, is a leading Darwinian scholar. With Adrian Desmond, he coauthored *Darwin* (Time/Warner Books, 1991), the best-selling, critically acclaimed account of the great evolutionist's life and times.

CHARLES DARWIN

1

A "GOOD-FOR-NOTHING" SON

Not for the first time, Dr. Robert Waring Darwin warned young Charles about his casual attitude. The doctor had worked hard to build a successful medical practice, like his father's before him, and shrewd investments had made him rich. His son, he thought, was growing up to be a good-for-nothing country squire with no occupation, who would fritter away his inheritance on horseback riding and the pleasures of "an idle sporting man." "You care for nothing but shooting, dogs, and rat-catching," he said, "and you will be a disgrace to yourself and all your family." No, it just would not do; Charles must get serious and plan a career for himself.

Charles thought his father was being much too tough on him, but he couldn't deny the facts. (Besides, few people ever argued with Dr. Darwin, a stern, non-stop talker, whom Charles later called "the largest man whom I ever saw.") It was true that he loved bird-watching in the English countryside around his Shrewsbury home in Shropshire, near the Welsh border. Often he came home dirty and scratched, his boots soaked from the morning dew or caked with mud from the river banks. Certainly, he would have to plead guilty to cherishing a beetle collection that was his pride and joy; at the age of 13, he had even described, in a scientific journal, a new species he had "captured" in the neighborhood. And yes, he was inordinately curious about the fish and frogs he netted from the River Severn, which flowed right by The Mount, his family's home. A skillful shot, he sometimes popped birds with his rifle and often jammed his pockets full of strange-looking minerals. "I was born a naturalist," he decided later. But he certainly couldn't

Doctor Robert Darwin, a prosperous English physician, had hoped his son Charles would also become a doctor of medicine. (Courtesy American Museum of Natural History)

tell the formidable Dr. Darwin, all six feet and 350 pounds of him, that he really wanted to keep doing these things for the rest of his life, so he said the expected words. He told his father not to worry, that he would study medicine and apply himself to becoming a physician. Of course, he hoped he could also be an amateur naturalist on the side, like his grandfather Erasmus—but first, he promised, he'd have a responsible career.

Dr. Robert Darwin delivered his stern lectures almost daily, usually after supper. When he held forth for hours on the subject of his own opinions, no one in the household dared to interrupt. He harangued Charles constantly, but he wasn't a mean man, just a very concerned one. He was genuinely worried about his son's future. Charles's mother had died when the boy was only eight years old, and the busy doctor feared he had not been able to provide enough parental guidance to his two sons and four daughters. Certainly, as a member of a well-off, though not aristocratic, family, young Charles was well cared for by nannies and servants. And Caroline, one of his three older sisters, helped raise him. Dr. Darwin was satisfied that his son was growing into a bright and well-mannered young lad with an amiable disposition, but Charles just seemed to be having too much fun playing sportsman and naturalist to care about his own future. At the Shrewsbury School, he paid little attention to his Latin and Greek lessons, and it seemed impossible that he would acquire the necessary preparation for medical school. Not that he didn't show an interest in science—he did, but it was the kind of science that resulted in loud explosions when he and his brother Erasmus (who was named after their grandfather) attempted some ill-conceived chemical experiments. (For years afterward, his brother called him "Gas"— the first of his many nicknames.)

Charles had his heroes, but they weren't doctors. Of course, he was impressed, as was the entire Darwin family, with his grandfather Erasmus's achievements, not only as a physician but also as a philosopher, naturalist, and poet. Erasmus Darwin's books *Zoonomia* (1794–1796), *The Temple of Nature* (1803), and *The Botanic Garden or Loves of the Plants* (1789) were famous. Charles also admired his cousins the Wedgwoods, with whom the Darwins had been close for generations. His grandfather's best friend had been Josiah Wedgwood, the man who made a fortune in industrial pottery and ceramics in England, and later created the world-renowned Wedgwood china. Charles's father had married Josiah's daughter, Susannah Wedgwood, and never remarried after her death. Charles adored his "Uncle Jos," the second Josiah Wedgwood, a kindly man of ample talents and achievements.

Charles's real idols, however, were the great naturalists and travelers he knew only in imagination, from reading their books. By the time a few more years had passed, these heroes would include Georges Cuvier (1769–1832), the great French zoologist; Carl Linnaeus (1707–1778), the Swede who classified thousands of plants and animals; and Alexander von Humboldt (1769–1859), a German explorer who traveled over much of the world making discoveries, from Humboldt's penguin to the Humboldt current. The German naturalist's vivid, meticulous journals of his voyages to South America were full of scientific contributions won at the expense of dangerous adventures. Charles didn't dare mention to his father that these were the kinds of careers he envied. There were hardly any jobs in natural science at which a gentleman, however talented, could expect to earn a living, and Charles could easily imagine the paternal outrage such an announcement would provoke.

Charles was quick-witted and hungry for knowledge about the world, but his studies at Shrewsbury School were a complete bore. "The school as a means of education to me was simply a blank," he recalled as an adult. "I learned absolutely nothing except by amusing myself reading and experimenting with chemistry." Looking back later in life, he thought that his father and all his teachers had considered him "a very ordinary boy, rather below the common standard of intellect." But that really was not true. "They all tell me you are very clever," his father once taunted him in an argument about money; most adults who met young Charles recognized his keen mind, but gave him no praise because he simply refused to apply himself to what they considered important.

If he did not excel at his Greek textbooks and had no interest in hearing the schoolmaster drone on about classical poetry, he did have several childhood passions that only a lucky few carry with them to adulthood: an intense curiosity about the natural world and how it came to be, a sense of wonder and delight toward living things, a thirst for discovery and adventure, and a packrat's love of collecting unusual objects. He was curious about how many eggs each kind of local songbird laid, and climbed trees to find out (first making a rule that he would collect only one egg from any nest).

He was intrigued by the behavior of insects and once became totally lost by the side of a road watching processions of ants, oblivious to a royal carriage rolling by; he sought out the homes of foxes and hedgehogs and wondered how many earthworms it would take to bury a large boulder in the earth.

As for the collector's mania, he had it as strongly as any child who hoards and catalogs baseball cards or Marvel comics in our own time. Beetles were his favorites, but he also collected bird eggs, shells, minerals, fossils, the artistic seals that were then impressed on documents and letters, and coins from all over the world. And there was another boyhood love: adventure. He dreamed of going to sea, of visiting exotic lands, of climbing mountains, exploring jungles, and sailing among tropical islands half a world away from the sleepy English countryside he knew so well.

Dr. Darwin enrolled Charles in Dr. Butler's Shrewsbury School in 1818, when he was nine years old. (He had been born the same day as Abraham Lincoln: February 12, 1809.) For the next seven years, Charles ignored the Greek and Latin lessons, and ran home each day to tend his treasured collections and read his books on travel and natural history. Finally, his father decided that "he was doing no good at school" and it was time to get on with the medical career—the third generation of Doctors Darwin. Charles was sent to the University of Edinburgh, in Scotland's capital, which was a world-class center for training physicians. Trying hard to live up to his father's expectations, Charles almost convinced himself that a medical career would suit him, even though he knew he wouldn't need to earn money, for "father would leave me property enough to subsist on with some comfort." In preparation for his life as a gentleman country doctor, he listened to his father's advice on how to set up a practice, followed him on his rounds, and showed some talent for healing when he spent a summer vacation as a volunteer, tending the local poor who could not afford a doctor.

In 1825, when he was 16, he set off for the University of Edinburgh. His older brother Erasmus was just completing his own medical course there. (Erasmus never practiced and instead became a gentlemanly dabbler in literature and the arts.) For two years, Charles dutifully ground his way through the courses in anatomy and curative plants and herbs, which he found unbearably dull. He wrote to his sister Caroline of "the long stupid lectures" he had to endure, such as one "cold, breakfastless hour on the properties of rhubarb." Charles found a hated professor "so very learned that his wisdom has left no room for his sense," and disliked another's classes "so much that I can not speak with decency about them." Yet he held his own, determined not to fail and disappoint his father.

What finally made it impossible for him to continue were the shockingly brutal surgical procedures he was expected to learn. By today's standards, professional surgeons of the nineteenth century practiced crude butchery. Since general anesthetics had not yet been invented to put patients into a deep sleep, the most prized skill in a good surgeon was lightning speed in cutting. Could he saw an infected leg off a man who was fully awake in less than two minutes? If not, the patient was likely to bleed to death or suffer fatal shock to his system, not to mention excruciating pain. The need for cleanliness and antiseptics was not yet understood, so even after successful operations, patients were likely to become infected. As a student observer, Charles was unable to bear the screams of a strapped-down child during major surgery; he ran out of the operating theater horrified, abandoning all thoughts of a medical career.

Even while studying medicine in Edinburgh, however, Charles found time to pursue his old hobbies. A few men who shared his interest in natural history took him to local scientific societies, where he met others who loved geology and zoology as much as he did. One of the professors of zoology, Robert Edmond Grant (1793–1874), took him on field trips to a Scottish bay with a wonderful name, the Firth of Forth, where he became fascinated by the tidepool creatures.

One day, when Charles was walking with Dr. Grant, the professor expressed his high admiration for the French zoologist Jean-Baptiste de Lamarck and his book on evolution. Darwin "listened in silent astonishment." Evolution—the idea that species of plants and animals change over time and are all related through common ancestors—was almost a Darwin family secret. Outside of his grandfather Erasmus's writings, people in polite society were expected to accept on faith that God created each living "kind" separately and instantly. Charles was too startled and embarrassed to say anything; his grandfather's evolutionism was notorious, but Charles had always allowed the creationist views held by most of his friends and teachers to go unchallenged.

It was also in Edinburgh that he met the talented taxidermist John Edmonston, a black man who had formerly been enslaved in South America, and who now made his living stuffing animals. Charles paid him for professional lessons in how to mount birds and mammal specimens for his collection.

Geologists in Edinburgh had long been inspired by the remarkable cliffs on the outskirts of their city, which are packed with fossils of ancient life. It was no accident that some of the greatest early geologists were Scots who knew the Edinburgh area—men like James Hutton, Charles Lyell, and later Hugh Miller. It was great fun for a curious young naturalist to explore this geological treasure trove. Each time he split open a rock with his geologist's hammer, he anticipated the thrill of perhaps gazing upon a creature no human had seen before, an organism that hadn't been exposed to the light of day for many thousands of years. (Today, we would say millions of years, but when Charles Darwin was young, few had any idea that the Earth was that old.) By contrast, Charles found the geology lectures he attended at the university so "incredibly dull" that he resolved "never as long as I lived to read a book on geology." However, during holidays at home he loved to hunt local rocks with an elderly amateur geologist, Mr. Cotton, whose enthusiasm turned a walk into an adventure.

The interests that had held Charles's attention since childhood—geology, the study of rocks; zoology, the study of animals; botany, the study of plants; and, to a lesser extent, astronomy, the study of the heavens, and travelers' accounts of tribal peoples—were all loosely lumped together under the heading "natural history." In the early 1800s, there was an enormous popular craze for the subject. Exotic plants and animals drew great crowds, stimulating the establishment of municipal zoos and museums of natural history throughout the nineteenth century.

A person who studied natural history was called a naturalist, although most early naturalists were simply collectors. Like childish postage stamp collectors, their passion was to acquire rare specimens others didn't have. The "mob of naturalists without souls," Charles later called them, for they showed little interest in using their collections to discover "scientific laws of life." By his mid-twenties, Charles would graduate from "mere collecting" to trying to understand why there are so many different varieties of very similar creatures, like beetles, and whether species were sharply distinct or blurred into one another. He wondered how they were adapted to their environment, how they behaved and reproduced, and he began to keep notebooks to organize information and focus his thinking, a process that eventually turned him into a "philosophical naturalist" or "natural philosopher," like his grandfather.

Old Erasmus Darwin had gathered a great deal of evidence to support his belief that all plants and animals were related through common ancestors. He was, in fact, the first naturalist to publish a detailed theory of evolution, although several had previously entertained the idea. Never having known his grandfather, who died in 1802, Charles believed himself to be relatively uninfluenced by him, but Erasmus's views were firmly embedded in the Darwin family's tradition. Charles absorbed them as part of his upbringing. Fifty years before Charles was born, Erasmus was investigating and writing about questions that would later occupy his grandson's attention: the theory of descent with modification (later known simply as evolution); how selective breeding of plants and animals creates new varieties; natural camouflage; animal instincts; and movement in plants, among many other topics.

Erasmus possessed tremendous curiosity. His boyhood interest in collecting fossils later expanded into every branch of natural history. Eventually, his writings on medicine, botany, and zoology earned him election to the Royal Society, Britain's most prestigious scientific organization—making him the first of six generations of Darwins to receive that honor. But it was the bread-and-butter side of his grandfather's life that Charles was expected to follow. After graduating from Cambridge, Erasmus had studied medicine at Edinburgh, then moved back to England, where he established a prosperous practice as a country doctor among the well-to-do.

Some of the most brilliant and inventive men of Erasmus's day had lived not far from his home, near the town of Lichfield, and he became a ringleader in bringing them together for the fun of sharing their scientific interests. Among the men were inventor James Watt, industrialist Matthew Boulton, chemist Joseph Priestley, and potter Josiah Wedgwood—all of them prime movers in creating the technology that took England into the industrial era.

Erasmus helped found the Lunar Society, which brought these lighthearted notables together regularly. The "Lunatics," as they called themselves, met only during full moons, so that they might find their way home in their horse-drawn carriages by bright moonlight. Their conversations were probably among the most interesting in England during the 1780s—of Watt's steam engine or Wedgwood's new ceramic methods, of Priestly's oxygen experiments or Erasmus Darwin's theories about how plants and animals originated.

Erasmus devoted much of his writing to two major questions: whether all living things are related through common ancestry, and by what means one species might develop into another. He assembled evidence from comparative anatomy, embryology (the study of an individual's development before birth), the geographical distribution of plants and animals, and the study of fossils. In his massive two-volume *Zoonomia, or the Laws of Organic Life* (1794–1796), Charles's grandfather had written that in the "millions of ages before the commencement of the history of mankind . . . all warm-blooded animals have arisen from one living filament" with the "faculty of continuing to improve . . . and of delivering down these improvements by generation to its posterity, world without end!"

While rejecting the biblical idea that each species was created instantly and separately, Erasmus did not lose respect for "the Author of all things." It was just as wonderful, he argued, that "the Cause of causes" had set the whole evolving web of life in motion. Always the optimist, he believed evolutionary development made continual progress toward ever greater perfection in all the productions of nature.

Charles's half-hearted attempt to follow in the medical footsteps of his father and grandfather had ended in failure. After the abrupt termination of that career, Charles did not relish the thought of returning home to face his father's daily tirades. Dr. Darwin, now 61, was almost ready to hand over his practice to his sons, but now neither of them wanted to be physicians. Charles could not bear to tell him the disappointing news; his sisters handled the thankless task.

Charles took refuge with his Uncle Jos at the Wedgwood home called Maer Hall, at Staffordshire, about 20 miles from his father's home at Shrewsbury. At Maer he was under no pressure, for "life there was perfectly free," as he later recalled, and there were evening parties filled with music. He was able to go out shooting birds to his heart's content in the surrounding countryside and to enjoy the company of the young Wedgwood women, including his cousin Emma. One of Josiah's sons, Hensleigh, who was six years older than Charles, was a favorite companion, often accompanying Charles on hiking and hunting trips. Uncle Jos was very fond of Charles and took him on tours of Scotland, Ireland, London, and Paris—more "idling" that left Dr. Robert Darwin stewing.

What was to be done with this bright, likeable son who seemed to lack a direction in life? Dr. Darwin had seen plenty of spoiled rich young men who squandered their family's money on horses, hounds, drinking, and gambling, never marrying or doing anything useful with their lives. He had tried to educate his son in good schools, but Charles had only wasted the tuition money and his professors' time. At the age of eighteen, he was still shooting partridges with his uncle's friends and spending long hours in the woods and fields, pausing to examine every flower, insect, and rock.

Finally resigned to his son's odd behavior, Dr. Darwin tried to find another occupation in which Charles could be respectable and respected, perhaps do some good in the community, and still be able to tramp around the countryside as an amateur naturalist. The answer he came up with was the church: Charles could be a country clergyman, as were several of his relatives and cousins. It was a purely practical decision, since Dr. Darwin was not a religious man—if anything, he was a freethinker who did not believe the Bible, but, as he later confided to Charles, that was something he never discussed with anyone. It was not the next world Robert Darwin was concerned about but how to get along in this one. He reassured Charles that he need not commit himself to an ascetic life of self-denial, nor study theology and Bible verses all day. Typically, an English country parson was a graduate of Oxford or Cambridge who married a wealthy wife and had a large family. He was an important and respected man in the village, welcome in the homes of the biggest landowners, and their frequent guest at lawn parties, hunts and sporting events. If he was also a large landowner, this combination squire and parson, or "squarson," lived in a large rectory, which was tended by a few servants and gardeners. Part of his time might be spent as a local magistrate, judging local court cases and helping keep order in the district. It was a privileged life with light duties "that left room for much else besides—a little shooting, a little drinking, a little doubt, and, if one liked, a good deal of natural history."

When Dr. Darwin told Charles that being a clergyman would give him a respectable excuse to continue tramping about the countryside, the idea appealed to the young man. Charles had been reading the Reverend John Sumner's *Evidences of Christianity* (1824) and other books on religion. "As I did not then in the least doubt the strict and literal truth of every word of the Bible," Charles wrote later, "I soon persuaded myself that our Creed must be fully accepted." Dr. Darwin sent his son off to Cambridge, paid the bills, and hoped for the best.

Again, Charles could not keep his mind and his efforts on what he was supposed to be doing. His cousin, Darwin Fox, who was also studying to be a clergyman at Cambridge, had a passion for collecting beetles, and the two of them often spent hours combing the nearby fields and woods for specimens. "No pursuit at Cambridge," he wrote years later, "was followed with nearly so much eagerness or gave me so much pleasure as collecting beetles . . . One day, on tearing off some old bark, I saw two rare beetles and seized one in each hand; then I saw a third and new kind, which I could not bear to lose, so that I popped the one which I held in my right hand into my mouth. Alas it ejected some intensely acrid fluid, which burnt my tongue so that I was forced to spit the beetle out, which was lost, as well as the third one."

However, beetles aside, he accomplished little at Cambridge along the lines that his father had wanted. During Charles's three years there, "my time was wasted as far as the academic studies were concerned as completely as at Edinburgh and at school." He fell in with a sporty set of young men who spent their days riding and shooting and their evenings drinking, knowing "that I ought to feel ashamed of days and evenings thus spent."

He also passed some time enjoying good music, appreciating fine paintings in the museums, and reading literature and poetry. But as usual, his heart was with natural history, and several older scholars befriended him, particularly the Reverend Adam Sedgwick, a geology professor, and the Reverend John Henslow, a botanist who was to play a major role in Charles's life. Both men were of the type he had intended to become: clergymen-naturalists.

Although self-taught, Henslow was very knowledgeable in geology, botany, and entomology, the study of insects. When he came to Cambridge no degrees were given in natural history subjects, a situation he determined to change. He revived the university's moldering herbarium (a reference collection of dried plants), refurbished its natural history museum, replanted its botanic garden, and helped make scientific learning respectable in an institution long dominated by Greek and Latin classics and theology, the study of religious philosophy.

Professor Henslow favored "hands-on" experience with living things. He took his students on high-spirited spring field trips into the countryside, where he showed them how to ask nature, rather than books, for answers. "Nothing could be more simple, cordial, and unpretending than the encouragment which he afforded to all young naturalists," Charles later recalled. Never flaunting his vast knowledge, he put the young men perfectly at ease, treating their questions and blundering "discoveries" about flowers or insect behavior with the same respect he gave accomplished senior professors. Honest mistakes were corrected "so clearly and kindly that one left him in no way disheartened, but only determined to be more accurate the next time."

By the time Charles returned home from Cambridge in 1831, without having completed his training for the clergy, Henslow's encouragement had transformed him from a boyish beetle collector into a budding naturalist, with a special interest in learning geology—a subject he had thought, from lectures, was too boring to ever catch his interest. But reading Humboldt's new journals about his visit to Tenerife in the Canary Islands had fired Charles's enthusiasm. Even while his father was attempting to push him back on course toward a career in the Church of England, Charles was busily making plans for a geologizing trip, first to Wales and then to Tenerife with Professor Henslow, which pleased neither Mrs. Henslow nor Dr. Darwin. Charles wrote to his sister Caroline:

> *All the while I am writing now my head is running about the Tropics: in the morning I go and gaze at Palm trees in the hot-house and come home and read Humboldt: my enthusiasm is so great that I cannot hardly sit still on my chair . . . Henslow promises to cram me in geology.—I never will be easy until I see the peak of Tenerife and the great Dragon tree; sandy, dazzling plains, and a gloomy silent forest, are alternately uppermost in my mind. —I am working regularly at Spanish; Erasmus advised me decidedly to give up Italian. I have written myself into a Tropical glow.*

When Henslow bowed to his family responsibilities and canceled the trip to Tenerife, he encouraged Charles to join the Reverend Adam Sedgwick's geologizing trip to Wales instead. Called "the first of men" by his friends (a gentle pun on his first name), Sedgwick was also a great teacher and took a special interest in Charles's development as a geologist. The two of them enjoyed a brief, happy field trip in Wales collecting rocks during the month of August. However, Charles decided he must get back to Uncle Jos's house at Staffordshire by the first of September, because "I would have thought myself mad to give up the first days of partridge shooting for geology or any other science." Could anyone blame Dr. Darwin for being about ready to burst?

But then something unexpected and dramatic appeared that was to change Charles's life—and the course of scientific discovery— forever. It was a letter.

CHAPTER 1 NOTES

p. 1   "an idle sporting man" *Autobiography,* p. 56.

p. 1   "You care for nothing . . ." *Autobiography,* p. 28.

p. 1   "the largest man . . ." *Autobiography,* p. 29.

p. 2   "I was born a naturalist" *Correspondence,* 2, p. 440.

p. 4   "The school as a . . . simply a blank" *Autobiography,* p. 27.

p. 4   "a very ordinary boy . . ." *Autobiography,* p. 28.

p. 4   "They all tell me . . ." *Autobiography,* p. 72.

p. 5   "father would leave me property . . ." *Autobiography,* p. 46.

p. 6   "the long stupid lectures . . . cold breakfastless hour . . . so very learned . . . so much that . . ." CD to Caroline Darwin, Jan. 6, 1826. *Correspondence,* 1, p. 25.

p. 6   "listened in silent astonishment." *Autobiography,* p. 46.

p. 7   "never as long as I lived . . ." *Autobiography,* p.52.

p. 8   "mob of naturalists without souls . . ." CD to H.W. Bates, Nov. 20, 1863, *CD Life and Letters,* ii, p. 393.

p. 9   "millions of ages before . . ." and ". . .delivering down these improvements . . ." *Zoonomia* i, 505; *Erasmus Darwin,* p. 71.

p. 10   "life there was . . ." *Autobiography,* p. 55.

p. 11   "that left room for much else . . ." J. R. Moore, "Darwin of Down," in David Kohn, ed., *Darwinian Heritage,* pp. 435–483.

p. 11   "As I did not . . ." *Autobiography,* p. 57.

p. 11   "No pursuit . . . one." *Autobiography,* p. 62

p. 12   "my time was wasted . . . evenings thus spent" *Autobiography,* p. 58.

p. 12   "Nothing could . . . so clearly and kindly . . ." CD in Nora Barlow, *Darwin and Henslow,* pp. 221–222.

p. 13   "All the while I am writing . . ." CD to Caroline Darwin, April 26, 1831. *Correspondence,* p. 122.

p. 13   "I would have thought myself mad . . ." *Autobiography,* p. 71.

2
"A USELESS UNDERTAKING"

On his way to joining Uncle Jos's annual fall partridge hunt, Charles stopped off at his father's home in Shrewsbury. Waiting for him there was a recent letter from Professor Henslow, dated 24 August 1831. Henslow, Charles's favorite professor, had been asked to help Capt. Robert FitzRoy find a naturalist for his surveying ship, the HMS *Beagle*; its mission was to explore and chart the coastline of South America, then continue on around the globe to survey longitudes. Henslow explained that the captain was seeking a young man to serve as ship's naturalist—not a "mere collector," he stressed, but a gentleman who would also be an intelligent companion for the captain. "I consider you to be the best qualified person I know of who is likely to undertake such a situation," Professor Henslow wrote. "I state this not in the supposition of your being a *finished* naturalist, but as amply qualified for collection, observing and noting, anything worthy to be noted in Natural History . . . Don't put on any modest doubts or fears about your qualifications, for I assure you I think you are the very man they are in search of."

Henslow himself had, at his father's insistence, given up his own childhood dream of exploring African jungles and had settled instead for a quiet, unadventurous post at St. John's College, Cambridge. When FitzRoy's letter arrived, it rekindled Henslow's deferred dream of wandering through tropical rain forests, and he thought of joining the *Beagle*'s expedition himself. This time his wife "gave her consent, but she looked so miserable" that Henslow knew he would not be sailing anywhere. It was his last, best opportunity to explore exotic lands, collecting strange plants and animals, and he hated to see it go to waste. He offered it first to his brother-in-law, the Reverend Leonard Jenyns, also a qualified naturalist, who was "so near accepting that he packed up his clothes." But Jenyns, almost a decade Darwin's senior and tied down down by church responsibilities, also had to decline. So Henslow urged young Darwin to seize the offer, as "there never was a finer chance for a man of zeal and spirit." Professor Henslow might at least be able to share in his student's adventure, even if only from half a world away.

But when Charles broached the subject to his father, the doctor came down on him hard. He denounced it as foolish, hare-brained—"a wild scheme" no man of sense would approve. To Dr. Darwin, it was just another attempt to escape the responsibility of preparing for a sensible career. Associating with sailors would be destructive to his character, and disreputable for a future clergyman. And there must be something wrong with this situation if the captain was willing to take someone so young and inexperienced. Most probably, there was something wrong with the ship and they could not find anyone truly qualified who would take the position. Charles had better forget all about it, and return to Cambridge to finish his exams for a clergyman's degree.

Charles dutifully wrote back to Professor Henslow, with regrets, that he could not accept the offer. But he was brokenhearted. His father, he thought, was standing in the way of his chance of a lifetime, his dream of exploring the world, of seeing the wonders he had only read about. Still, he would not defy his father's wishes.

To a stubborn young lad with a wanderlust, Dr. Darwin may have seemed a tyrannical ogre, blocking his son's heart's desire. But Robert Waring Darwin, who lived with the pain of having become an early widower, was also a protective father who loved his bright, adventurous son and feared losing him forever. Many young men had shipped out from England during its heyday of exploration and never came back, killed in ocean storms or by tropical diseases. Malarial areas of Africa and South America were commonly known as "the white man's graveyard," and the *Beagle* was of a design sailors had nicknamed "floating coffins" or "half-tide rocks" because they went down so easily in foul weather.

Dr. Darwin could not have known the *Beagle*'s history at the time, but his gut feeling was well founded. During her first surveying expedition along the rough, stormy coastline of Patagonia (1826–1830), the *Beagle* barely managed to remain afloat, let alone accomplish her mapping missions. By 1829, she was in poor repair and out of provisions, with most of her crew so debilitated by scurvy and disease that they were unable to work. Capt. Pringle Stokes struggled valiantly, but finally gave in to despair, and shot himself in the head. Then the ship was assigned to young Lt. Robert FitzRoy, who almost lost her in a violent storm soon after taking command. Dr. Darwin's fears were well justified.

Although his father had laid down the law about the voyage, Charles continued to search for even the smallest loophole. Perhaps if there were a mature person, someone his father respected, who thought this a good idea, might he be persuaded? "If you can find any man of common-sense who advises you to go," said Dr. Robert Darwin, "I will give my consent." It was a crack in the armor, and Charles went for it.

Early the next morning, Charles took a buggy and traveled the twenty miles to Maer, the Wedgwood place. Breathlessly, he told his cousin Hensleigh the opportunity that had been offered and how his father had made him turn it down. Hensleigh protested that it was a terrible decision, and suggested they speak with Uncle Jos immediately. Maybe he could turn the doctor around.

Uncle Jos puffed his pipe and listened patiently as Charles recounted Professor Henslow's letter and reported the doctor's decision. He saw the disappointment in his nephew's eyes, and listened while Hensleigh pleaded that Charles must be allowed to join the *Beagle* expedition.

After a long pause, Uncle Jos asked Charles if he had seriously considered the hardships and risks of such a voyage. Did he really understand that he might be killed in a storm or shipwrecked—particularly in the treacherous waters off southern South America? Charles replied that he did not take the dangers lightly. There were many, he knew, who had gone to sea and never came back. And then he talked on and on about how it was the chance of a lifetime. To travel around the world! To see the tropics! No longer could his father complain that he was lazy or idle. There would be so much to do: keeping notes and journals; collecting, identifying and cataloging thousands of specimens; learning the ways of shipboard; studying books on geology, botany, and zoology. He would see coral islands, overgrown jungles with monkeys and parrots, savage tribes, all the wonders he had read and dreamed about! Whatever the risks, he would be perfectly willing to accept them.

Uncle Jos was convinced that his nephew was prepared, but the boy's father most definitely was not. However, he felt that Charles was sufficiently grown up to shape his life according to his own decisions. It was time for Dr. Darwin to let go, worrisome as that may be to him. Uncle Jos offered to write at once, or even to drive back to Shropshire, to convince him not to hold Charles back.

Charles handed his uncle a list that he had jotted down of Dr. Darwin's reasons why the voyage would be a bad idea. The first, main objection was that the voyage would be "disreputable to [his] character as a clergyman," to which Mr. Wedgwood replied: "The pursuit of Natural History, though certainly not professional, is very suitable to a clergyman." He answered each objection in turn, down to the last: "that it would be a useless undertaking." Here Charles's uncle showed his real understanding and appreciation of his nephew. "Looking upon Charles as a man of enlarged curiosity," he wrote, "it affords him such an opportunity of seeing men and things as happens to few."

Charles sent Uncle Jos's letter off to his father, with a note adding that he would abide by the doctor's final decision and would "never mention the subject again." Rather than wait for a reply, Charles and his uncle took a carriage back to Shrewsbury to confront his father. Faced with Josiah's enthusiasm, Dr. Darwin caved in: Charles could go on the voyage, and the doctor would pay all his expenses.

Meanwhile, Captain FitzRoy had invited an old friend of his to share his cabin, so there was now no room for Charles. At the last minute, however, the friend declined, and the position was open once again. Darwin traveled to London to see FitzRoy, and found the captain aristocratic, gentlemanly, interested in science, and sure of his command, even though he was just four years older than Charles.

"He offers me to go share in everything in his cabin if I like to come," Charles wrote home, "and every sort of accommodation that I can have, but they will not be numerous . . . There is something extremely attractive in his manners and way of coming straight to the point . . . He thought it his duty to state everything in the worst point of view . . . He says I must live poorly—no wine, and the plainest dinners . . . If I do not choose to remain with them, I can at any time get home to England. . . . He asked me at once, 'Shall you bear being told that I want the cabin to myself—when I want to be alone? If we treat each other this way, I hope we shall suit; if not, probably we should wish each other at the Devil." Darwin also wrote to Professor Henslow, "Captain FitzRoy is everything that is delightful . . . You can not imagine anything more pleasant, kind, and open than Captain FitzRoy's manners were to me."

Since British captains were expected to remain aloof from their hired crews, FitzRoy was looking for an independent gentleman companion with whom he could discuss science, philosophy, and theology—as well as a ship's naturalist. A surgeon was serving as "official" ship's naturalist, but FitzRoy wanted a younger, "unofficial" one on board as well. A believer in the pseudo-sciences of physiognomy and phrenology, FitzRoy was convinced he could read people's abilities from their facial features or bumps on their heads. Noting Darwin's shapeless, squidgy nose, he thought it revealed a lack of energy and determination. (FitzRoy himself had sharp, angular features.) However, after interviewing Charles, he decided that this enthusiastic Cambridge-educated gentleman would make an intelligent cabin companion and "messmate," though his nose might not win any prizes. Darwin had no such misgivings and judged FitzRoy "my beau ideal of a captain." After becoming friends, they sometimes joked about the captain's "faith in Bumpology."

So greatly did the two young men affect the course of each other's lives that FitzRoy is often remembered only as "Darwin's captain." However, he would have made his mark in any event—as seaman, explorer, surveyor, mapmaker, meteorologist, and, later, governor of New Zealand.

A staunch believer in the literal interpretation of Scripture, FitzRoy never could have imagined that his vessel was to become famous as the birthplace of evolutionary biology. In fact, one of the things he hoped for the voyage was that he would find geological evidence for Noah's Flood and perhaps contribute to proving the truth of the biblical account of Creation.

Born in Suffolk to the aristocratic Graftons, whose lineage descended from an out-of-wedlock son of King Charles II (1630–1685), Robert FitzRoy's relatives included courtiers, admirals, sea

Robert FitzRoy, whose last name means "son of the king," was an aristocratic officer, brilliant navigator, and captain of HMS *Beagle*. (Courtesy New York Public Library)

captains, and Lord Castlereigh, a prime minister. (His family name is from the French *fils roi* meaning "son of the king.") Trained for command at the Royal Naval College at Portsmouth, he graduated with top honors, then served on several vessels, which took him to the Mediterranean and to South America.

In 1828, then-Lieutenant FitzRoy was given command of the *Beagle*, a 21-gun brig which had been sent to map the frigid and desolate southern coasts of South America, including Patagonia and Tierra del Fuego. Despite the rough weather and short supplies, FitzRoy roused the dispirited crew to carry forward its surveying and exploration. It was during this first command of the *Beagle* (1828–1830) that FitzRoy became obsessed with the Indian tribes of Tierra del Fuego. Although they lived in a harsh climate, these small, sturdy people went nearly naked; they painted their bodies, hunted and fished with very simple tools, and appeared to the Englishmen almost as beings from another planet.

These natives, among the poorest people on Earth, were awed by the English ships and prized its little whaleboats, which were far superior to their own dugout canoes. Stealthy raiding parties of Fuegians would slip aboard the ship by night to steal the whaleboats, which infuriated the captain. During one violent confrontation, the crew fought back and chased them to shore, where one Fuegian was shot dead by an officer. After about a dozen Indians had been captured, FitzRoy decided to hold them as hostages. However, the tribesmen, showing complete indifference to their kinsmen's fate, still refused to return the boats. After a week or so of stalemate, FitzRoy released them all—except a nine-year-old girl who did not want to leave the ship. FitzRoy named her Fuegia Basket and decided to teach her English.

During subsequent encounters with the Indians, FitzRoy "acquired" three more Fuegian youths, young men whom he considered just a cut above wild animals. ("Scarcely superior to the brute creation," was how the captain phrased it.) One was given the name York Minster, another Boat Memory, and the third—a bright, personable young lad—was called Jemmy Button. According to some accounts, FitzRoy bought him with a fancy mother-of-pearl button from his uniform, though the captain claimed he gave it to the boy's father as a souvenir.

FitzRoy, in a grandiose and well-intentioned—but ultimately arrogant—scheme, intended to take these young "savages" to England, where he would save their heathen souls. They would be taught "English, and the plainer truths of Christianity," reading,

Jemmy Button, one of the native Fuegians brought back to England to be "civilized," as sketched by Capt. Robert FitzRoy. (Author's collection)

gardening, and "the use of common tools." In the captain's view, they would be lifted from the ignorance of their primitive culture and raised to the heights of British civilization. FitzRoy then planned to return them three years later to their homeland, where they could teach what they had learned, including the English language, to all the other Indians. Their fellow tribesmen, he reasoned, would be so eager to learn from them that soon the entire coast would emerge from heathen darkness into the light of Britannia. From then on, whenever His Majesty's sailors were shipwrecked on this treacherous coast, they could count on English-speaking Indians to come to their assistance, and perhaps even offer them a civilized luncheon of some shepherd's pie and a spot of tea.

Soon after reaching England, however, Boat Memory contracted smallpox and died, perhaps because of a faulty vaccination. FitzRoy took great care to see that the other three Indians were maintained in good health and enrolled in a Missionary Society School. Jemmy Button and Fuegia Basket, at least, were good pupils, whose progress attracted attention in the press. In the summer of 1831, FitzRoy was summoned by King William and Queen Adelaide to bring the Fuegians to Court. Wearing his kid gloves and shiny boots, Jemmy made a great hit. The Queen even gave Fuegia Basket one of her own bonnets, a ring, and a purse filled with cash to buy clothes.

A few months later, FitzRoy grew anxious to take them back home, as he had promised. He petitioned the Admiralty several times, but its senior officers showed no interest in financing the project. Determined to keep his word, FitzRoy decided to take a year's leave of absence and return the Indians to South America at his own expense. After putting up the money to hire a ship, he was rescued by a politically connected uncle who finally persuaded the Admiralty to sponsor another surveying voyage for the *Beagle*.

She was commissioned to make extensive maps of uncharted territories, and was to carry a large cargo provided by the Missionary Society for the Indians' new life in Tierra del Fuego. The ship was to be manned by a crew of about 65, including 8 marines; in addition, there would be on board an artist, a surgeon, two missionaries, the three Fuegian Indians, a surgeon serving as ship's naturalist and the 22-year-old "unofficial" naturalist and messmate to the captain. Charles could hardly wait.

CHAPTER 2 NOTES

p. 15   "I consider you . . . the man they are in search of." J. Henslow to CD, August   24, 1831, *Correspondence,* 1, p.128.

pp. 15, 16 "gave her consent . . ." and "so near accepting . . ." CD to Susan Darwin, September 4, 1831. *Correspondence,* 1, p. 139

p. 16   "there never was a . . ." J. Henslow to CD, August 24, 1831. *Correspondence,* p. 129.

p. 16   "a wild scheme," *Autobiography,* p. 71.

p. 17   "If you can find any man of common-sense . . ." *Autobiography,* p. 71.

p. 18   " . . . a useless undertaking," CD to Robert Darwin. August 31, 1831. *Correspondence* 1, p. 133.

p. 18   "The pursuit of Natural History . . ." and "Looking upon Charles . . ." Josiah Wedgwood to Robert Darwin. August 31, 1831. *Correspondence,* 1, 133–134. Also, *Autobiography,* p. 229.

p. 18   "never mention the subject again." CD to Robert Darwin Aug. 31, 1831, *Correspondence,* 1, p. 133

p. 19   "He offers me to . . . Devil." CD to Susan Darwin September 5, 1831, *Correspondence,* 1, p. 140.

p. 19   "Captain Fitz-Roy is everything . . ." CD to J. Henslow, September 5 1831, *Correspondence,* 1, p. 142

p. 19   "my beau-ideal of a captain," CD to Susan Darwin, September 14, 1831, *Correspondence,* 1, p. 154.

p. 19   "faith in Bumpology," FitzRoy to CD, October 4, 1833, *Correspondence,* 1, p. 335.

p. 21   "Scarcely superior to the brute creation," Capt. Robt. FitzRoy to Capt. Philip King, September 12, 1830. *FitzRoy,* p. 53–54. Also, FitzRoy's *Narrative of Beagle,* 2, Chapter 1.

pp. 22–23 "English and . . . tools." *FitzRoy,* p. 57.

3

PAINTED SAVAGES AND GIANT TORTOISES

Charles was so excited about the voyage that he gladly accompanied Captain FitzRoy on a three-day round trip from London to Plymouth just to have a look at the ship that would carry them around the world.

The *Beagle* was lying in dry dock without her masts and sails, and Charles was surprised at how small she looked. A 242-ton brig reduced to 10 cannons, she had been practically rebuilt, with new fittings, her rotted woodwork repaired, and the officers' cabins paneled in shiny new mahogany. In whimsical contrast to the formidable artillery, her carved figurehead depicted the head and paws of a beagle dog. It was not an isolated example of the shipbuilder's sense of humor; other vessels in the fleet, with prow carvings that matched their names, were the HMS *Porcupine* and HMS *Opossum*.

Charles's work space was to be a tiny poop cabin above the ship's rudder, which had barely enough room for a table and a few drawers and shelves. He wrote Henslow that his cabin was "most woefully small. I have just room to turn round and that is all." He would have to keep his work supremely well organized or it would quickly bury him. Although only 90 feet in length, the *Beagle* would be home to approximately 70 people for five years, in fair weather and foul.

Nevertheless, a few weeks after seeing her, he wrote FitzRoy that he could hardly wait until the sailing date: "My second life will then commence, and it shall be as a birthday for the rest of my life."

That date was December 27, 1831. Just prior to sailing, during Christmas week, some of the crew had gotten drunk and brawled in port. Charles observed a British captain's authority when Fitz-Roy ordered one sailor put in irons and others later flogged at sea. The *Beagle* set sail for the Atlantic, stopping first at the Cape Verde islands, then heading straight for the coast of Brazil, more than 3,000 miles to the southwest.

In the Cape Verdes, Charles explored Saint Iago, his first volcanic island ("that was a memorable hour for me"), which later inspired him to investigate the origin of such formations. While there, he visited isolated rocks full of great flocks of seabirds, boobies and terns ("of a tame and stupid disposition . . . I could have killed any number of them with my geological hammer") and daily cast his trawling nets for myriad sea creatures that he preserved, noted, and cataloged.

His constant companion was an overwhelming seasickness, which, he noted, caused a "misery . . . far beyond what I ever guessed at . . . nothing but lying in my hammock did any good." Early on, he made up his mind that he would not let it beat him and that he would never complain to FitzRoy—so he suffered in silence. Eventually he developed some tolerance to the rolling and pitching, but for the next five years, seasickness was never far from him. He already suffered, too, from symptoms of an unknown illness that may have first appeared shortly before the voyage, and which grew gradually worse, perhaps with added complications, during his stay in the tropics. Even today, at a distance of more than a century and a half, historically-minded doctors—including allergists, psychiatrists, and experts in tropical diseases—still puzzle and argue over the nature of Darwin's mysterious malady and when it first appeared.

Young Charles Darwin's gritty determination to collect specimens and record observations, despite daily bouts of weakness and nausea, earned him the crew's respect. Even the captain said he had never seen a "shore-going" man adapt so quickly and easily to shipboard life. Of course, some officers objected to his constantly cluttering their decks with the rocks, slimy sea creatures, and other "rubbish" he collected, earning him the new nickname of "Flycatcher."

On crossing the equator, Charles received the traditional initiation sailors liked to bestow on first-time travelers to the tropics. FitzRoy, dressed as King Neptune with a scraggly seaweed beard, ordered several others to seize the young man, smear his face with paint and thick tar, and then "shave" off the gooey mess with a saw blade. Finally, they tossed Charles into a sail full of saltwater and bounced him around in it—amid raucous laughter. The usually strait-laced captain tolerated this horseplay, knowing it helped buoy the men's spirits during their difficult and dangerous expedition.

The ship was making good time, and about two months out of England she reached the Brazilian port of Bahía—a beautiful old town near the edge of the rain forest. Charles was impressed by the luxuriant tropical plants around the streets: bananas, oranges, coconuts, and sweet-smelling jasmine. When he ventured into the nearby wilderness, he said, he felt like a blind man who has just been given eyes, gazing with delight on scenes out of the Arabian Nights. "Delight itself, however, is a weak term to express the feelings of a naturalist who, for the first time, has wandered by himself in a Brazilian forest," he wrote in his journal. "The elegance of the grasses, the novelty of the parasitical plants, the beauty of the flowers, the glossy green of the ferns and general luxuriance of the vegetation, filled me with admiration . . . Such a day brings a deeper pleasure than [I] can ever hope to experience again."

Even more than the awe-inspiring beauty of the place, the riotous life forms in the rain forest presented more interesting spectacles than his eye could follow or his mind grasp. There was so much to see he could barely take a step without being overwhelmed. He wrote on February 28, 1832:

> The delight one experiences in such times bewilders the mind; if the eye attempts to follow the flight of a gaudy butterfly, it is arrested by some strange tree or fruit; if watching an insect one forgets it in the stranger flower it is crawling over; if turning to admire the splendour of the scenery, the individual character of the foreground fixes the attention. The mind is a chaos of delight, out of which a world of future & more quiet pleasure will arise.

The *Beagle* continued southward down the Brazilian coast, and by the first week of April 1832 sailed into the magnificent harbor at Rio de Janeiro. It was a busy port, with a distinctive forest of tall masts, bustling with slave laborers loading cargos of bananas and coffee onto the clipper ships.

Slavery sickened and infuriated Darwin—the more so because he felt totally powerless to intervene. He heard the pitiful cries of a young Brazilian serving girl coming from an old Portuguese woman's house. This slave owner regularly crushed her servant's fingertips in screw-vises for the smallest infractions. Years later, the girl's screams still echoed in Charles's nightmares.

Once he and the captain got into a bitter argument about slavery. FitzRoy was an excellent seaman and a charismatic commander, but he could also be imperious and arrogant. When contradicted, he flew into rages. FitzRoy claimed that enslaved Africans preferred to live within the plantation system because they knew they were better off under their master's protection. Darwin insisted that no man or woman would remain a slave if given a choice.

At FitzRoy's request, a Brazilian plantation owner gathered his slaves together and asked them whether they would rather be free. All said that they were contented with their lot, and FitzRoy crowed to Darwin that his case had been proved. "I then asked him," Darwin wrote, "perhaps with a sneer, whether he thought that the answers of slaves in the presence of their master was worth anything. This made him excessively angry, and he said that if I doubted his word, we could not live any longer together."

Despite these occasional flare-ups, however, relations between the two were good, and Darwin was chosen to accompany FitzRoy on many of his overland expeditions. Darwin also traveled through the interiors of Brazil, Chile, and Argentina, where he was bitten by the Benchucha bug—a carrier of the debilitating Chagas' disease. He may have become infected, for young Darwin was quite different from the older, semi-invalid philosopher of later years, who tired easily and daily suffered headaches, abdominal pain and vomiting. As a young man, he thought nothing of trekking 400 miles through hostile Indian territory, or of climbing unexplored mountains. (Several were named after him, including Mount Darwin, on an island in Tierra del Fuego, Chile; the Darwin Mountains in Patagonia; and Mount Darwin, South Africa, which is also the name of a district.)

Back in England, Charles's father was, in his peculiar way, finally trying to get into the spirit of the voyage. Dr. Darwin wrote that he had gotten a banana tree in honor of his son's adventures in the tropics. "It flourishes so as to promise to fill the hot-house. I sit under it, and think of you in similar shade." Somewhat later, the doctor admitted in a letter to Professor Henslow: "I thought the voyage hazardous for his happiness but it seems to prove otherwise."

While FitzRoy worked out the exact longitude of Rio de Janeiro and made the first accurate maps of the South American coastline, Charles collected exotic mammals, birds, plants, reptiles and invertebrates, including hundreds of species new to science. Later he hacked fossil skeletons of giant sloths and armadillos out of cliffs and studied the composition of coral islands and reefs. Neither storms, earthquakes, wars, nor volcanic eruptions deterred him; he viewed them all as phenomena to be studied, grist for his mill.

His boyhood love of collecting was now unleashed in many directions, but few excited Charles as much as gathering the mineralized bones of extinct, giant animals. He was not even sure what sorts of creatures they were and wondered what the experts would say. Even his old hunting joys paled beside the thrill of stalking prehistoric beasts. "The pleasure of the first day's partridge shooting," he wrote home, "cannot be compared to finding a fine group of fossil bones, which tell their story of former times with almost a living tongue." Also, these giant sloths and armadillos—so similar to the much smaller versions living in South America today—surely were clues to a large question that had begun nagging at him, the same riddle that had obsessed his grandfather: how did species originate?

It was an endless parade of wonders. For Charles, it was to be five years of adventures, hardships, scientific discovery, and difficult, unremitting work. During the voyage, he was able to store up more first-hand information about the world than most of us can cram into a lifetime. He had galloped on horseback alongside Argentinian *gauchos,* hitched a ride on a pony-sized tortoise, and wandered awestruck through creeper-laced rain forests teeming with gaudy birds and exquisite orchids. To another traveler, these events and experiences might register as striking but unrelated impressions. What was remarkable about the *Beagle*'s young naturalist was that he habitually sought underlying connections and regularities. It was only some years after returning home, however, that he realized the key to it all: a grand view of life evolving on a changing Earth, with humans sharing only the last few moments of an immense history.

Henslow, his old professor, remained Charles's land-bound partner on the voyage. From Brazil, Darwin wrote, "The delight of sitting on a decaying trunk amidst the quiet gloom of the forest is unspeakable and never to be forgotten. How often have I then wished for you." His teacher replied, "Your account of the Tropical forest is delightful. I can't help envying you."

Henslow took on the burden of receiving the endless crates and boxes of rocks, plants, and preserved mammals, birds, insects, and fish that Darwin shipped home. Each one was carefully opened, damaged specimens removed, and every item carefully arranged and stored. Henslow also offered detailed advice and guidance to the inexperienced young naturalist; Darwin had taken on an enormous job and was at first unsure whether he was collecting "the right facts." Professor Henslow reassured him that he was.

Darwin's brushes with danger came more from people than from the sea or forest. In Argentina, he found himself in the midst of a bloody, horrendous war of genocide. The ruthless General Manuel Rosas was enthusiastically exterminating the Pampas Indians so that cattle ranchers could take over their land. "I believe such a villainous Banditti-like army was never before collected together," Charles noted in his journal. When he presented himself to the Argentinian military, as all strangers were required to do, Charles identified himself as a naturalist. "What means this naturalista?" a suspicious commandant had demanded. Darwin's traveling companion replied in Spanish, "A naturalist is a man who knows about everything." "Aha," said the officer, "A spy!" It took some hasty explaining for them both to leave with their necks intact—and with a document guaranteeing safe passage for "Don Carlos Darwin, Naturalista." Back in England, after learning of this incident, Dr. Darwin named his hothouse banana tree "the *Don Carlos* tree, in compliment to you."

HMS *Beagle* **is hailed by Fuegian tribesmen near the southern tip of South America. Similar ships capsized so frequently that sailors nicknamed them "floating coffins."** (Courtesy American Museum of Natural History)

Before Darwin could rejoin the *Beagle,* he received a note from his captain, expressing hopes that the dangerous inland expedition had gone well:

> *How many times did you flee from the Indians? How many precipices did you fall over? How many bogs did you fall into? How often were you carried away by the floods? And how many times were you kilt?*

When Darwin and the *Beagle*'s crew finally reached the cold, rough waters near the southern tip of South America, FitzRoy was anxious to see Darwin's reaction to the Fuegian Indians. To the captain, their very existence was "disagreeable, indeed painful" to contemplate. But "unwilling as we may be to consider ourselves even remotely descended from human beings in such a state, the reflection that [Julius] Caesar found the Britons painted and clothed in skins, like these Fuegians" excited FitzRoy's hopes. What a triumph if his "experiment" to civilize these "savages" could succeed!

Darwin never forgot his first view of the Fuegians. He described a group of them "partly concealed by the entangled forest . . . perched on a wild point overhanging the sea . . . It was without exception the most curious and interesting spectacle I ever beheld. I could not have believed how wide was the difference between savage and civilized man." They reminded him of the grimacing, crouching devils he had seen on an Edinburgh opera stage, but these were absolutely naked; one woman even nursed her baby in the cold sleet, which "fell and thawed on her naked bosum, and on the skin of her naked baby! These poor wretches were stunted in their growth, their hideous faces bedaubed with white paint, their skins filthy and greasy, their hair entangled, their voices discordant, their gestures violent . . ." Still, he was impressed with York Minster's and Jemmy Button's personable brightness, amazed that such agreeable shipmates could have come from these "miserable, degraded savages." Was the gap really so great as it appeared? "I do not think that our Fuegians were much more superstitious than some of the sailors," Darwin had to admit, "for an old quarter-master firmly believed that the successive gales were caused by our having the Fuegians on board."

The Fuegians were finally returned to their homeland, with the missionary Richard Matthews, to begin teaching their adopted civilization to their kinsmen. With them, the sailors left dozens of crates of items donated by the Missionary Society back in London: beaver hats, tablecloths, fine white linens, tea trays, silver soup tureens. Darwin thought it a ridiculous waste, totally impractical in this harsh environment. ("The choice of articles showed the most culpable folly and negligency," he wrote.) But Matthews had also brought seed for vegetable gardens, gardening implements, and tools for building huts.

Soon after the *Beagle* departed, the local Fuegians attacked the new settlement, stole everything, beat up Jemmy Button, and almost killed Father Matthews. When the ship returned weeks later, Darwin and FitzRoy found only a pathetic remnant of their experimental colony. York Minster had run off with the young woman Fuegia Basket and all Jemmy's goods and clothes. FitzRoy's hopes and plans for spreading the light of civilization seemed to be smashed.

In the Fuegian fiasco, in the oppression and brutality of slavery, and in General Rosas's relentless slaughter of the Pampas Indians—as well as in the daily life-or-death dramas he observed among wild creatures in the oceans and forests—Darwin began to see everywhere a "struggle for existence." Just beneath the cathedral-like harmony of rain forests, the cultural diversity of tropic peoples, or the calm of a Pacific lagoon, there seemed to be a constant testing of every plant and creature. Any small advantage it could gain—a defensive poison, a concealing color, the production of more offspring—might make the difference between survival and extinction.

Off Chile, in 1835 the voyagers narrowly missed being caught in a very spectacular and destructive earthquake. Three volcanoes in the Andes erupted on the same night, setting off massive tremors throughout the area. Charles wrote his sister Caroline:

We are now on our road from Concepcion. The papers will have told you about the great Earthquake of the 20th of February. I suppose it certainly is the worst ever experienced in Chile. It is no use attempting to describe the ruin—it is the most awful spectacle I ever beheld. The town of Concepcion is now nothing more than piles & lines of bricks, tiles & timbers—it is absolutely true there is not one house left habitable . . . The force of the shock must have been immense . . . the ground is traversed by rents . . . [thick buttresses] are broken into fragments like so much biscuit. How fortunate it happened at the time of day when many are out of their houses [or] very few would have escaped to tell the tale. . . . I am very glad we happened to call at Concepcion so shortly afterwards . . . It is indeed most wonderful to witness such desolation produced in three minutes of time. . . .

Here Charles could actually watch geologic features change, practically before his eyes. "A bad earthquake at once destroys our oldest associations," he wrote, "the earth, the very emblem of solidity, has moved beneath our feet like a thin skin floating on liquid—one second of time has created in the mind a strange idea of insecurity, which hours of reflection would not have produced." The coast looked "as if a thousand ships had been wrecked," but Darwin was even more impressed by the resultant elevation of the land. "There can be no doubt that the land round the Bay of Concepcion was upraised two or three feet," he wrote.

"Captain FitzRoy found beds of putrid mussel-shells still adhering to rocks [that were now] ten feet above the high-water mark." Fuegian "savages," the tropical rain forest, and the Chilean earthquake, Darwin concluded, were "the three most interesting spectacles I have beheld since leaving England."

More remarkable observations were in store for Charles when the *Beagle* briefly visited the Galapagos Islands in September 1835. After two unsuccessful attempts to navigate around Cape Horn (almost capsizing the vessel in rough waters) FitzRoy had steered through the Straits of Magellan. About 600 miles west of Equador, poking out of the deep Pacific Ocean, were a cluster of volcanic cones: the Galapagos Archipelago.

Five main islands, and a scattering of smaller ones, pierce the water astride the equator. Early Spanish sailors called them *Las Islas Encantadas,* the Enchanted Isles: miniature, self-contained worlds of desert, scrub, misty forest, and black volcanic beach. Darwin and the HMS *Beagle* spent only five weeks exploring them in September and October of 1835, but the islands made a lasting impresssion. The diversity of Galapagos wildlife was a real delight to the young ship's naturalist. Large tortoises and lizards dominated the landscape; aside from shipborne mice and rats, there were no land mammals. Along with the prehistoric-looking iguanas, he encountered penguins, dolphins, seals, bright red crabs, a bewildering array of mockingbird and finch species, and the incredible giant tortoises, from whose saddle-shaped backs (*galapagos* is "pony saddle" in Spanish) the islands were named. Despite the marine iguana's fearsome, dinosaurian appearance, he soon learned that they are vegetarians, diving to the ocean bottom to graze on seaweed. (Darwin cut open a dead one's stomach to discover that fact.)

As for the tortoises, they were so docile that whaling ships routinely visited the Galapagos to carry the creatures off for their larders. It took six or eight men to lift one, but a single animal could yield 200 pounds of meat. In Darwin's day, sailors, pirates, and whalers took more than 200,000 of the great reptiles to help feed crews on long voyages. Hundreds were dumped, live, into ship's holds for months, awaiting their turn to become soup. Mariners, perhaps to assuage their own guilt, had a legend that when a wicked naval officer died, he was forced to return as a giant tortoise.

Because of their long isolation, the Galapagos animals had never developed any fear of man. The finches, wrens, mockingbirds, doves, and even carrion buzzards—like the tortoises and seals—had an "extreme tameness." "A gun is here almost superfluous," Darwin wrote, "for with the muzzle I pushed a hawk off the branch of a tree." The former bird-hunting boy from Shropshire was astonished at the contrast between this trusting disposition and that of the birds back in England, which had apparently learned to flee from humans thousands of years ago. Two years later, he wrote his sister Caroline to ask their father, "Is it in [grandfather Erasmus Darwin's] *Zoonomia* or notes to *Botanic Garden* where there is a passage about acquired instincts, such as crows learning Guns are dangerous?"

On Darwin's last day in the Galapagos, the governor of an island mentioned that he could identify any of the giant tortoise shells Darwin had collected, according to the island from which it came. Darwin was astonished; it had not occurred to him that these closely clustered islands could have anything but the same species of tortoises, finches, or iguanas on all of them. Only later, back in England, when the bird expert John Gould was helping sort out his collections, did Charles realize that this time he had not collected "the right facts." He had not bothered to carefully tag many of the Galapagos specimens with the names of the particular islands from which they came! At the time, there seemed no reason to do so. Later he would realize that "all observation must be for or against some view if it is to be of any service."

Three years later, with hindsight, and an evolutionary theory, he looked at the Galapagos creatures all over again—and the view was very different. He would revise his *Journal* in 1839 to read: "The natural history of these islands is eminently curious, and well deserves attention. Here, both in space and time, we seem to be brought somewhat near to that great fact—that mystery of mysteries—the first appearance of new beings on this earth." Other naturalists had made him realize that Galapagos plants and animals were unique—found nowhere else in the world. Even more surprising, each island was inhabited by a different set of species.

Each speck of an island, it turned out, had its own special kind of giant tortoise, mockingbird, or finch. "I never dreamed that islands—about fifty or sixty miles apart, and most of them in sight of each other, formed of precisely the same rocks, placed under a quite similar climate, rising to a nearly equal height—would have been differently tenanted." Yet all the various species on the little islands "show a marked relationship with those of [South] America, though separated from that continent by an open space of ocean."

In fact, the Galapagos Archipelago is a compact little model of how the whole planet may have been populated by radiating species adapting to different ways of life and descended from common ancestors. Darwin was later to write that the distribution of species in the Galapagos, together with the fossils of giant extinct sloths and armadillos he found in South America, were "the factual origin of all my views."

But it was the diversity of closely related species on the several islands that Darwin said "strikes me with wonder." Indeed, there were 13 types of finches, each with a different type of beak, from delicate to heavy, from small to large. "Seeing this gradation and diversity of structure in one small, intimately related group of birds," he wrote, "one might really fancy that from an original paucity of birds in this archipelago, one [ancestral] species had been taken and modified for different ends."

In the revised version of his *Journal*, Darwin concluded that the Galapagos "is a little world within itself, or rather a satellite attached to America, whence it has derived a few stray colonists . . . Considering the small size of these islands, we feel the more astonished at the number of their aboriginal beings, and at their confined range . . . the different islands to a considerable extent are inhabited by a different set of beings . . . One is astonished at the amount of creative force, if such an expression may be used, displayed on these small, barren and rocky islands."

The *Beagle* visited Tahiti and the Society Islands, then continued on to New Zealand, Australia, and Tasmania, to Keeling Island and Mauritius in the Indian Ocean, and to the Cape Colony in South Africa. Then, instead of heading north to England (to the chronically seasick Darwin's dismay), the *Beagle* traced the eastern coast of South America once more before returning home.

On the last leg of the voyage, Darwin constructed a theory of how coral reefs were formed. He had taken with him the newly published *Principles of Geology* (1830–1833) by Sir Charles Lyell. Volume one had been a parting gift from his mentor, Professor Henslow, who advised Charles to read it for its facts, but "on no account to accept" its new theories. What Henslow considered revolutionary in Lyell's *Principles* was the "uniformitarian" approach to understanding geological features. Most churchmen-geologists up to that time had argued that the Earth's major mountains, continents, and deserts had been shaped rapidly by catastrophes and forces unlike any known to science.

Opposing this traditional "catastrophic" view, Lyell argued that the Earth's features were created gradually through erosion, sedimentation, the action of glaciers, and gradual accumulations of lava flows—processes that could be observed still operating all over the planet. Before long, Darwin said, he was forming theories that "came half out of Lyell's brains" and was seeing things "through his [Lyell's] eyes." Whenever Darwin explored a rocky island or climbed a mountain, he looked for clues to the "small causes" active today that can produce major geological changes over immense periods of time.

While on the west coast of South America, Darwin had noted that the shorelines seemed to show evidence of having been both repeatedly built up and subsequently worn down. That gave him an idea of how coral reefs might be formed, although he had yet to see one.

At Tahiti in November 1835, he made his first field studies of reefs, and described three types: atolls, which are circular and enclose a lagoon; barrier reefs, which are long walls near a coastline, separated from the land by a channel; and fringing reefs, which stretch along a shoreline. All are built by tiny soft-bodied animals of the jellyfish family that live in colonies by the billions. Each secretes a protective limestone cell around itself, which makes up the hard structure of the coral.

Darwin's theory of coral reefs began with his observation that live corals grow only in shallow water. He combined that with the observation that reefs seem to be associated only with areas of subsidence (land that is settling or sinking.) Where there is uplift, as in the vicinity of volcanoes, atolls and barrier reefs do not occur.

Basic reef formation, he deduced, is caused by the coral animals building on the limestone base of former colonies, where the shore is subsiding. Since it thrives only in shallow water, the colony keeps growing upward to maintain itself at the same depth, while the ground beneath it keeps sinking. It was a perfect demonstration of Lyell's "uniformitarianism"; given enough time, small, persistent natural forces create major geological features. Some reefs are indeed over a thousand feet thick; cores drilled deep within them have long since confirmed that Darwin's explanation was essentially correct. (We now know, too, that world sea levels have been rising for thousands of years.) His first strictly scientific book, *The Structure and Distribution of Coral Reefs* (1842), was well received by scientists.

Darwin recorded the water temperatures near reefs, and analyzed the natural community of plants and animals that forms around them. He realized that corals are keystone species; they modify the environment, providing food and shelter for many other creatures. Darwin's grasp of this web of interrelationships later inspired his German disciple Ernst Haeckel to coin the term ecology, meaning the study of an organism's relationship to its environment (from the Greek *oikos,* a home.)

Shortly after his return to England, Charles would become fast friends with his idol in geology, Charles Lyell, whose books had been such eye-openers during the voyage. To Darwin's delight, Lyell would agree that he really had discovered how coral reefs are formed. After their meeting, his mentor wrote: "I could think of nothing for days after your lesson on coral reefs, but of the tops of submerged continents . . . It is all true, but do not flatter yourself that you will be believed, till you are growing bald, like me with hard work & vexation at the incredulity of the world."

Just before *Coral Reefs* was published, Darwin's journal, popularly known as *Voyage of the Beagle* (1839), appeared, and was critically acclaimed as a great traveler's narrative. It would win Charles his first fame, but he had come perilously close to losing the manuscript forever. For safekeeping, he had sent the only copy home on a ship that sank at sea. Its cargo was rescued, however, and the precious journal eventually reached the Darwin family. "We are now reading it aloud," his sister wrote while he was still on the last leg of his voyage, "and Papa enjoys it extremely except when the danger you run makes him shudder."

First published as the last of a three-volume report, with the full title *Journal of Researches into the Geology and Natural History of the Various Countries Visited by H.M.S. Beagle Under the Command of Captain FitzRoy, H.M.N. From 1832 to 1836,* Darwin's volume alone was a best-seller, while the others, including one written by FitzRoy, were read only by specialists.

Many years later, Sir Arthur Conan Doyle, the creator of Sherlock Holmes, praised Darwin's *Voyage of the Beagle* as one of the best books about "travel and the frequent heroism of modern life." (His other choice was Alfred Russel Wallace's *Malay Archipelago,* about which we will hear more later.) Doyle admired Darwin's "gentle and noble firmness of mind" and devotion to his naturalist's quest:

> *Nothing was too small and nothing too great for . . . alert observation. One page is occupied in the analysis of some peculiarity in the web of a minute spider, while the next deals with the evidence for the subsidence of a continent, and the extinction of a myriad animals . . . [Darwin] rode the four hundred miles between Bahia and Buenos Ayares, when even the hardy Gauchos refused to accompany him. Personal danger and a hideous death were small things to him compared to a new beetle or an undescribed fly.*

There had been discoveries, excitement, and adventures enough to last Darwin a lifetime. Now he was ready to settle down, perhaps find a wife, and spend the rest of his life trying to sort out his thousands of impressions and observations—not to mention the organization and publication of his vast collections.

Charles always referred to his strenuous voyage of discovery as "my first real education." Nevertheless, after five years at sea, the quiet, green English countryside he had fled began to gain in attractiveness. Longing for home, he wrote his sister Caroline that his seafaring days were over:

> *The voyage has been grievously too long; . . . I continue to suffer so much from sea-sickness, that nothing, not even geology itself, can make*

up the misery & vexation of spirit. But . . . the very thought of [seeing you all again] shall drive sea sickness & blue sea devils far away . . .

People are pleased to talk of the ever smiling sky of the Tropics: must not this be precious nonsense? Who admires a lady's face who is always smiling? England is not one of your insipid beauties; she can cry, & frown, & smile, all by turns.—In short I am convinced it is a most ridiculous thing to go round the world, when by staying quietly, the world will go round with you.

On October 2, 1836, the *Beagle* made its safe return to Falmouth, England. It was a very different Charles Darwin who made his way back to the families of his father and Uncle Jos. Charles was now a man to be reckoned with in the scientific world, a rising young naturalist whose collections had created a stir at the Royal Society and the British Museum. Top zoologists, botanists, and geologists would vie to work on his collections. He had survived hardships and dangers, proved himself resilient and self-reliant, and certainly could no longer be accused of laziness. Although he had come back from the tropics with a mysterious ailment, his personality was now strong and self-assured. Sir Charles Lyell had told a pleasantly astonished Dr. Robert Darwin that the world could expect "great contributions" of his son.

When at last Robert Darwin saw his wandering boy again, he did notice that something seemed quite different about him, but couldn't quite put his finger on it. "Why, the shape of his head is quite altered," the doctor finally announced. It wasn't, of course: what had taken on new dimensions was the mind inside.

CHAPTER 3 NOTES

p. 25   "most woefully small . . ." CD to J. Henslow, October 30, 1831, *Correspondence,* 1, p. 176.

p. 25   "My second life will . . ." CD to Robert FitzRoy, October 10, 1831, *Correspondence,* 1, p. 175.

p. 26   "that was a memorable hour . . ." *Autobiography,* p. 81. "of a tame and . . . hammer," *Voyage of Beagle,* p. 10.

p. 26   "misery . . . did any good." CD to Robert Darwin, March 1, 1832, *Correspondence,* 1, p. 201.

p. 27   "Delight itself, however . . . experience again." *Voyage of Beagle,* p. 12

p. 27   "The delight one experiences . . ." *Beagle Diary,* for February 28, 1832, p. 39.

p. 28   "I then asked him . . . any longer together." *Autobiography* p. 74

p. 29   "It flourishes so . . . in similar shade." Robt. Darwin to CD, March 7, 1833, *Correspondence,* 1, p. 301.

p. 29   "I thought the voyage . . ." Robt. Darwin to J. Henslow December 28, 1835, *Correspondence,* 1, p. 473.

p. 29   "The pleasure of . . . living tongue." CD to Catherine Darwin, April 6, 1834, *Correspondence,* 1, p. 379.

p. 30   "the right facts," CD to J.S. Henslow, May 18, 1832, *Correspondence* 1, p. 236.

p. 30   "I believe . . . collected together." *Voyage of Beagle,* p. 70

p. 30   " . . . naturalista?" *Voyage of Beagle,* p. 82; *FitzRoy's Journal* for August 22, 1832, (1977 ed.) p. 82.

p. 30   *"Don Carlos tree" Correspondence* 1, p. 274.

p. 31   "How many times . . . were you kilt?" FitzRoy to CD, October 4, 1833, *Correspondence,* 1, p. 334.

p. 31   "disagreeable . . . unwilling as . . . these Fuegians," FitzRoy's Journal (1977 ed.), p. 102

p. 32   "partly concealed . . . civilized man." *Voyage of Beagle,* pp. 204–205

p. 32   "fell and thawed . . . gestures violent . . ." *Voyage of Beagle,* December 25, 1832, p. 213.

p. 32   "I do not think . . . on board." *Voyage of Beagle,* p. 216.

p. 32   "The choice of articles . . ." *Beagle Diary,* p. 129.

p. 33   "We are now . . . three minutes of time." CD to Caroline Darwin, March 10, 1835. *Correspondence,* 1, pp. 433-434.

pp. 33–34 "A bad earthquake . . . produced." "There can be . . . above the high water-mark." CD to Caroline Darwin, March 19, 1835. *Correspondence,* 1, p. 432.

p. 34   "the three most interesting spectacles . . ." CD to Caroline Darwin, March 10, 1835. *Correspondence,* 1, p. 432.

p. 35   "A gun is here . . ." *Voyage of Beagle,* October, 1835, p. 399.

p. 35   "Is it in *Zoonomia . . .*" CD to Caroline Darwin, May 19, 1837, *Correspondence,* 2, p. 19.

p. 35   "all observation . . . any service." CD to Henry Fawcett, September 18, 1861 *Correspondence,* 9, p. 232.

p. 35   "The natural history . . . on this earth." *Voyage of Beagle,* September 1839, p. 378.

p. 36   "I never dreamed . . . ocean." *Voyage of Beagle,* p. 394.

p. 36   "the factual origin of all my views." Journal entry for June 26, 1837 in *Correspondence,* 2, p. 431.

p. 36   "Seeing this gradation . . . modified for different ends." *Voyage of Beagle,* p. 381.

p. 36   "is a little world . . . rocky islands." *Voyage of Beagle,* p. 398.

p. 37   "on no account to accept . . ." *Autobiography,* p. 101

p. 37   "came half out of Lyell's brains . . . through his eyes." CD to L. Horner, Aug. 29, 1844, *Correspondence* 3, p. 55

p. 38   "I could think of nothing . . . incredulity of the world." Charles Lyell to CD, Feb. 13, 1837, *Correspondence* 2, p. 4.

p. 39   "We are now reading . . ." Susan Darwin to CD, November 22, 1835, *Correspondence,* 1, p. 469.

p. 39   "Nothing was too small . . . undescribed fly." Sir Arthur Conan Doyle, *Through the Magic Door,* p. 245–246

pp. 39–40 "The voyage has been grievously . . . far away." CD to Caroline Darwin, March 10, 1835. *Correspondence,* 1, pp. 433–444.

p. 40   "People are pleased . . . round with you." CD to Caroline Darwin, July 18, 1836, *Correspondence,* 1, p. 501.

p. 40   "the shape of his head is quite altered . . ." *Autobiography,* p. 79.

4

OF BRIDES AND BARNACLES

While Charles was away, there had been some changes among the young people in the Darwin and Wedgwood clans. Charles's older sister Caroline had married Uncle Jos's son, also known as Jos Wedgwood. "I am very glad of the marriage for Caroline's sake, as I think she will be a very happy person, especially if she has children," Charles wrote to a friend, "for I never saw a human being so fond of little crying wretches, as she is. But I am an ungrateful dog to speak this way, for she was a mother to me, during all the early part of my life." By "crying wretches," he hastened to add, "I mean such little angels as all children doubtless are."

Does that sound like a young man who is just about to settle down and father ten children? Maybe not, but it was to be his last bachelor's potshot at what was in store for him. Charles's sisters had always tried to push him toward his cousin Fanny Wedgwood, who was plain and proper—a good wife for a clergyman—but she had died at the age of 26 while Charles was still at sea. Aside from another Wedgwood daughter, who suffered from birth defects, that left only Emma Wedgwood, an attractive, strong, and intelligent young woman, as an eligible bride for Charles.

It seems never to have occurred to Charles to look outside the family for a mate. From Dr. Darwin and Uncle Jos, there had been not-so-subtle pushing from the sidelines, but apparently not enough to scare the two young people away from each other. During the rounds of "welcome home" parties, Charles found a strong attraction growing between them.

With visions of a relaxed country life before him, surrounded, as he joked, by gardens, books, dogs, fireplace, and "a nice, soft wife," he suddenly proposed marriage to Emma on November 9, 1836. Uncle Jos and Robert Darwin were almost beside themselves with joy. Both took delight in further intertwining of the Wedgwoods and Darwins; no other families on Earth, it seemed to them, were worthy of receiving their offspring—or their inheritances. By the time the engagement was announced, all the relatives had been gossiping about the "chances & probabilities" of Charles and Emma getting married, but Caroline "was quite taken by surprise not thinking the event was so near taking place."

To his friend and geological mentor Lyell, Charles wrote, "I cannot avoid wishing to be the first person to tell Mrs. Lyell and yourself, that I have the very good, & shortly since, very unexpected fortune, of going to be married.—The lady is my cousin Miss Emma Wedgwood." When he announced their wedding date as only three months off, the gossipy Wedgwood sisters thought he was in too much of a hurry. "How I do wish he would . . . wait till Spring & fine weather! . . . It is the happiest time of Emma's life & it is a thousand pities it should be a very short one." Charles wrote Emma that "my father echoes and reechoes Uncle Jos's words: 'You have drawn a prize!'"

As he moved between London and the countryside, making arrangements for his wedding and his scientific collections, Charles dashed off amusing letters as part of his courtship song. Even a boring coach ride could be turned into a subject for Emma's entertainment. While respecting her sincerely held private religious beliefs, Charles cheerfully mocked those who put on public displays of holiness. His fellow travelers, he wrote, included "rather an elegant female . . . so virtuous that I did not venture to open my mouth to her." Before the vehicle departed, another lady instructed her, in a *very* loud voice, "to write to her either on Saturday night or Monday morning, Sunday being omitted in the most marked manner." After promising never to write on Sunday, and accepting her friend's shouted promise not to schedule prayers until the servants were awake, she spent the journey buried in a religious tract, "marking the best passages with a thick lead pencil . . . Her next neighbor was an old gentleman with a portentously purple nose, . . . and his next neighbor was the primmest

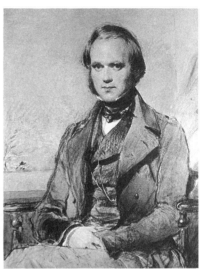

Back from his voyage, Charles Darwin posed for this pastel portrait, right, in 1839. Soon after, he and his cousin Emma Wedgwood, left, were married. (Courtesy American Museum of Natural History)

she-Quaker I have ever seen.—Was not I in good company?—I never opened my mouth & therefore enjoyed my journey."

"The question of houses,—suburbs versus central London— rages violently around each fireplace in this house," Charles wrote Emma. He warned her to "listen with much suspicion to all arguments in favour of retired places," because he was used to being "a solitary brute." Soon after his return, Charles had rented rooms in London near his brother Erasmus and spent much of his time at the British Museum, arranging and describing his collections. He also began searching for a suitable town house that he could share with his bride-to-be, but found "Houses are very scarce & the landlords are all gone mad, they ask such prices." In the meantime, he continued preparing his specimens, notebooks, and journals for publication.

"I miss a walk in the country very much; this London is a vile smoky place, where a man loses a great part of the best enjoyments of life," he wrote Emma. "I have seen no one for these two days; & what can a man have to say, who works all morning in describing hawks & owls; & then rushes out, & walks in a bewildered manner up one street & down another, looking out for the words 'To let'."

Finally, on January 29, 1838, Charles and Emma were married, and the next day moved to a house he had found on Upper Gower Street. There they stayed for two years while Charles found experts to take up the task of studying and publishing his collections, worked on his book about coral reefs, and prepared his diary of the *Beagle* voyage for publication as the *Journal of the Voyage of the Beagle.*

When it was time to start a family, the pull of the countryside was irresistible, and house hunting started all over again. In 1842, the Darwins bought a large Georgian home in the tiny village of Down (later spelled "Downe") 16 miles from London.

Despite its closeness to the city, Downe remains an isolated area even today, nestled in the gently sloping chalk hills ("downs") from which it takes its name. When the Darwins first moved there in the mid-nineteenth century, it retained the charm and social divisions of a medieval village. The community's largest land-

Home of the Darwins, Down House still stands in the village of Downe, near Bromley, about 16 miles south of London. Partially restored with its original furnishings, it is now the Darwin Museum. (Author's photo)

owner was their closest neighbor, Sir John Lubbock, a prominent London banker and noted amateur astronomer. (His son and namesake, John Lubbock, became Darwin's protégé.) Some of the local village folk were shopkeepers, gardeners, carpenters, and other support personnel for the few wealthy families. Village women still curtsied and men doffed their hats when such gentry as the Darwins rode by in their carriages. But although Charles and Emma moved in aristocratic social circles, they were of modest means compared to the wealthiest families of Downe.

Down House sits on 18 acres, including fields, a garden, and a clump of woods planted by Darwin and his gardeners. A sandcovered path wound through the shady woods and then returned toward the house along a sunny hedge-lined walk. Darwin called this sandwalk "my thinking path," and strolled it daily during breaks from writing.

Sometimes when deep in thought, he would stack a few stones around the turn in the walk. He might have a "three flint problem," just as Sherlock Holmes had "three pipe problems." Darwin would walk around the loop, knocking away one flint with his walking stick each time he passed. When all the stones were gone, it was time to head back home.

Here Darwin lived and worked for 40 years. At various times he added to the house, put a dovecote out back for his pigeon breeding experiments, and added a greenhouse (which still stands), a laboratory (now in ruins), and, later, a clay tennis court for his children. Charles and Emma raised their seven surviving children (three were lost to disease and birth defects) at Down House. Semi-restored as it looked a century and a half ago, with several of the rooms containing their original furnishings, it is open to the public today as the Darwin Museum and is near Bromley, a 20-minute train ride from London's Victoria Station.

In July 1837, a year after returning from his voyage of discovery, Charles began to keep notebooks on "the species question" to gather information "for or against" the idea that species evolve. He reread his grandfather Erasmus's books and found their ideas stimulating, but thought them long on speculation and short on facts. He had, of course, also read the French biologist Lamarck and would later peruse the anonymously written *Vestiges of*

Creation, which had enjoyed great popularity in England despite its mysterious authorship. (Only after the death of "Mr. Vestiges" was his identity revealed as Scots publisher and encyclopedist Robert Chambers.) Both books contained arguments for organic evolution, but Charles felt they fell far short of being convincing. Because of their uncritically compiled evidence and weak explanatory powers, neither had won acceptance by most expert naturalists of the day—although the public made it a best-seller.

Lamarck himself had written that "it is often harder to secure the recognition of a truth than it is to discover it." By 1846, Charles realized his fellow scientists would never take his own theorizing seriously unless he first mastered the details of some zoological group. With trays full of unclassified insects or barnacles before him, how could he decide which belonged to true species, which were variations within species, or which were evolving subspecies? Is there really such a thing as a species, or are apparent boundaries blurred in nature? To approach such questions, Charles devoted himself for eight years (1846–1854) to a painstaking study of barnacles, the little sea creatures that encrust dock pilings and ships' hulls.

Known to zoologists as Cirripedia ("curl-footed"), these marine invertebrates first held his attention when he discovered a new minute parasitic Chilean species that burrows into shellfish. When he found no place for it in the established classification, he reviewed the zoology of the whole group and realized it was in complete disarray.

Still a basic reference for specialists more than a century later, Darwin's four meticulous volumes on *Cirripedia* (1851–1855) brought accuracy and order to the study of all fossil and living barnacle species. In the course of the long, tedious work, he became a master taxonomist (classifier) and sharpened his understanding of species and their variability. At one point, Darwin wrote Captain FitzRoy that he was "for the last half-month daily hard at work in dissecting a little animal about the size of a pin's head . . . and I could spend another month on it, and daily see some more beautiful structure."

As the barnacle project dragged on for eight long years, Darwin wondered if it was taking him too far away from his research on the origin of species. About halfway through the work, he wrote to a friend, "I hate a Barnacle as no man ever did before, not even a Sailor in a slow-sailing ship." The Darwin children grew up accepting barnacle work as a regular part of life, as they had never seen their father do anything else. One of Darwin's young sons was once overheard asking a neighbor's child, "Where does your father work on *his* barnacles?"

After Darwin's death, his son Francis asked his father's old friend and colleague Thomas Henry Huxley if he thought the long barnacle project had been worthwhile, and received this reply:

> *Your sagacious father never did a wiser thing . . . Like the rest of us, he had no proper training in biological science, and it has always struck me as [a] remarkable . . . insight, that he saw the necessity of giving himself such training, and [courageous], that he did not shirk the labor . . . It was a piece of critical self-discipline, the effect of which manifested itself in everything your father wrote afterwards . . .*

Having proved himself as a "hod-carrier of science"—the workman who carries wheelbarrows full of concrete facts to bind the bricks of theory—Charles could at last return to the great questions that had buzzed in his mind since debarking from the *Beagle:* What is a species? Where did we come from? What are the laws of life?

CHAPTER 4 NOTES

p. 43   "I am very glad . . . doubtless are." CD to William Darwin Fox, July 7, 1837. *Correspondence,* 2, p. 29.

pp. 43–44 "a nice, soft wife." Notes on Marriage, July 1838. *Correspondence,* 2, p. 444

p. 44   "was quite taken by surprise . . . near taking place." Caroline Wedgwood to CD, November 11, 1838. *Correspondence,* 2, p. 114.

p. 44   "I cannot avoid . . . Emma Wedgwood." *Correspondence,* CD to Charles Lyell, November 12, 1838, *Correspondence,* 2, p. 114.

p. 44   "How I do wish . . . short one." Emma Wedgwood to Catherine Darwin, November 1838, *Correspondence,* 2, p. 115.

p. 44   "My father echoes . . . 'You have drawn a prize!'" CD to Emma Wedgwood, November 14, 1838, *Correspondence*, 2, p. 118.

pp. 44–45   "rather an elegant female . . . enjoyed my journey." CD to Emma Wedgwood, April 5, 1840, *Correspondence*, 2, pp. 261–262.

p. 45   "The question of houses . . ." CD to Emma Wedgwood, November 14, 1838, *Correspondence*, 2, pp. 117–118.

p. 45   "listen with much . . . a solitary brute." CD to Emma Wedgwood, November 14, 1838, *Correspondence*, 2, p. 118

p. 45   "Houses are very . . ." CD to Emma Wedgwood, November 27, 1838. *Correspondence*, 2, pp 128–129.

p. 45   "I miss a walk . . ." CD to Leonard Jenyns, April 10, 1837. *Correspondence*, 2, p. 15.

pp. 45–46   "I have seen no one . . . 'To Let'" CD to Emma Wedgwood, November 30, 1838, *Correspondence*, 2, p. 133

p. 47   "three flint problem" *CD Life and Letters,* i, p. 115

p. 48   "it is often harder . . . discover it." Lamarck, *Philosophical Zoology,* p. 404.

p. 48   "for the last . . . beautiful structure." CD to R. FitzRoy October 28, 1846. *Correspondence*, 3, p. 359.

p. 49   "I hate a barnacle . . ." CD to W. D. Fox, October 1852. *Correspondence*, 2, p. 100.

p. 49   "Where does your father . . ." *More Letters,* 1, p 38.

p. 49   "Your sagacious father . . . afterwards." *THH Life and Letters.* Vol I, p. 315.

p. 49   "hod-carrier of science," *CD Life and Letters,* i, p. 347.

5

A THEORY BY WHICH TO WORK

In 1837, two years after returning from his voyage of discovery, Charles decided to begin a "systematic enquiry" that might make sense of all he had learned and seen. Surely there was an order behind the "chaos of delight" he had experienced in the Brazilian forest, an organizing principle in back of the beetles and barnacles, giant sloth fossils, Galapagos tortoises and mockingbirds. He scrawled a challenge to himself: "The Grand Question, which every naturalist ought to have before him, when dissecting a whale, or classifying a mite, a fungus, or an infusorian, is 'What are the laws of life?'" His outward adventures were over, but the inner ones were just beginning.

He bought some special notebooks in which to jot down his wide-ranging collections of facts, thoughts, readings, and questions, all bearing on how species and varieties may have originated. Throughout his barnacle work, and while settling into family life at Down House, Charles pushed his thoughts and data onto paper. Somewhere along the line he realized his quest was the same as his grandfather's in *"Zoonomia; or the Laws of Organic Life"* (1794), which Charles now read again. The old book rekindled his fascination with evolution, which was then called "development" or "transmutation." He realized, however, that grandfather Erasmus had offered only a sprinkling of facts to support his grand conclusions. Charles's own father, Robert, leery of Erasmus's notoriety for airy theorizing (some called it "darwinising") had decided long ago he would never write anything except "answering questions about medicine" for his patients.

Charles titled one of his new notebooks "Zoonomia" and began filling it with evidence and questions bearing on "transformation." "If we let imagination run wild," he jotted, "then animals, our companions in work and amusement, and ourselves may be one— we may all be netted together." Charles had hundreds of questions: Are isolated island populations the most favorable for evolving new species? Why have many poisonous creatures evolved patterns of bright colors? But the most perplexing of all was still the *how* of evolution—what the great physicist John Herschel had referred to as "that mystery of mysteries": By what natural mechanism did species evolve? Neither Charles's grandfather nor such other early evolutionists as Lamarck or Chambers had come up with a plausible theory. More than 40 years later, in his *Autobiography*, Darwin wrote:

> *In October 1838, that is, fifteen months after I had begun my systematic enquiry, I happened to read for amusement [Thomas] Malthus On Population, and being well prepared to appreciate the struggle for existence which goes on from long- continued observation of the habits of animals and plants, it at once struck me that under these circumstances favourable variations would tend to be preserved, and unfavourable ones to be destroyed. The result of this would be the formation of new species. Here, then, I had at last got a theory by which to work . . .*

That statement about his moment of enlightenment, written many years later, oversimplifies Darwin's complicated route of discovery. Reading Malthus "for amusement" may have triggered a flash of insight, but only after years of systematic effort, during which the problem of "how the birds and beasts were formed" was constantly on his mind. Malthus's ideas would not have been new to him in 1838; from discussions with friends, he had been familiar with the Malthusian arguments long before he read them. Despite his own recounting of the "aha moment," scholars still argue over just how Charles arrived at his theory.

The Reverend Thomas Malthus's famous book described an alarming increase in population among the poor, and how their large families would lead to increased competition for limited resources. He argued that unchecked populations increase at a rate far beyond the food supply's capacity to keep pace. (This gloomy picture continues to haunt us, for the Malthusian time bomb of global overpopulation is still ticking. Today, however, it is more than a question of outstripping food resources. Human populations put immense pressure on habitats and global ecosystems, trigger changes in climate, and are causing extinctions of thousands of plant and animal species.)

Facts about competition for resources, and the so-called struggle for existence, however, made up only one important line of evidence. Given the limits of a human lifetime, where could Charles actually observe short-term evolution in action? He turned to the varieties of domesticated plants and animals that were being bred on Kentish country farms. He questioned his neighbors about their apples, hogs, and horses, and joined pigeon-breeding clubs. Few zoologists or naturalists would have looked to the ordinary barnyard for clues as to how nature works in deserts or rain forests. Charles took his information from wherever he could find it. How the camel got its hump or the elephant its trunk, he realized, were in the same class of problems as how the farmer could breed larger hogs or redder apples. Eventually, in 1868, he would publish a two-volume work on *The Variation of Animals and Plants Under Domestication,* summarizing all that was then known on the subject. But first, he used the facts he had gathered on domestic breeding to help build his case for evolution.

In science, the word "evolution" has come to have at least four distinct meanings: 1) the natural, ongoing process of species change (or change in populations below the level of a species, such as subspecies or varieties), whatever may cause it; (2) inevitable "progress" from lower to higher life forms, a notion discredited by Darwin himself; (3) the particular history of the "branching bush" of life, including the origins of various groups that are now reconstructed not only from the fossil record but also by biochemical studies; and (4) the mechanism or "engine" of evolution, which Darwin (and Alfred Russel Wallace, whom we shall soon meet) proposed as "natural selection."

Charles's idea of natural selection began with two facts he had seen everywhere in the natural world, observations that struck him at many times and places:

1. *Overproduction of individuals.* Most organisms produce many more offspring (or eggs or seeds) than will survive to reproduce themselves, as anyone who walks through the woods or dives near a coral reef can see.

2. *Variability among individuals.* All zebra foals or bullfrog tadpoles may look alike at first glance, but each one is unique. A naturalist studying thousands of individuals is struck by the wide range of variation within the same species—which a casual hiker or diver may *not* see.

Since many individuals leave no offspring, or very few, those that leave the most offspring will perpetuate their characteristics. Variations that bestow some advantage in a given environment will tend to be passed on. The popular notion that "survival of the fittest" means simply that strong "winners" kill off weak "losers" is a hopelessly distorted version of Darwinism. As Charles reviewed his field notes from the *Beagle* voyage, he was well aware that pressures may come from predators, climate, other members of an animal's social group (competing for space, food, or mates), or from parasites and disease.

Fossils, too, set his mind spinning with ideas about the origin of species. While in South America, his discoveries of a new kind of extinct giant sloth (*Mylodon darwinii*) and huge fossil armadillos fueled his fascination with paleontology, the study of ancient life. He found it especially interesting that these "monsters' bones" were found on the same continent where much smaller sloths and armadillos live today. Such distribution suggested that the prehistoric giants may have been ancestral—or at least ancient cousins—to the present species.

Evidence came, too, from embryology, the study of the development of creatures in the womb or egg. Nineteenth-century researchers could not distinguish between dog, calf, or human foetuses at early stages of their development; through crude magnifying instruments, they looked almost identical. To some researchers, embryos appeared to demonstrate all the transitional stages, like a speeded-up replay of their evolution. (We have since learned that developing embryos do not really summarize their species' history, except in a very general way.) Darwin saw an analogy between an individual's development and the evolution of species. Most people agreed that tadpoles turn into frogs and eggs into chicks by wholly natural processes, without divine intervention. He thought it strange that critics who claimed evolution is impossible had no trouble accepting the origin of individuals from sperm and eggs—a process that he thought no less remarkable.

Geology, of course, remained one of his major sources of evidence for the past history of the Earth and its inhabitants. As he had since his earliest days on the *Beagle,* Darwin continued to interpret rock formations through the lens of Lyell's principles: that geological changes occur slowly and gradually, over vast periods of time, caused by natural forces that can be observed operating today. In a sense, he had taken Lyell's "uniformitarian" ideas about the formation of mountains and coasts and applied them to living things—a daring step that Lyell himself was unwilling to take.

Charles continued to work in secret, gathering thousands of facts from these and other scientific fields to support his developing views, while carefully noting exceptions—the facts that didn't seem to fit. When he finally published his *Origin of Species* in 1859, critics complained that what was good in the theory was old, and what was new in it was wrong. Evolution itself was the "old" part, having previously been championed by Lamarck, Chambers, and Charles's grandfather Erasmus. The new part—natural selection—provoked the storm of criticism. Many people objected because the mechanism of natural selection contradicted their belief in a Divine Creator, who designed all species and created them instantaneously.

Charles began arguing his case by showing how farmers and pigeon breeders had evolved domestic varieties gradually, through "artificial" selection.

Natural selection, he explained, was in some ways similar to the "artificial" selection practiced by farmers. Neither form of selection can *create* variability; both merely act on the differences between individuals that nature constantly produces. (How genetic inheritance works eluded Darwin all his life, and only became generally known after 1900.) Farmers and pigeon hobbyists are only able to select the variations they can see, while nature itself "can act on every internal organ . . . on the whole machinery of life." And while domestic animal breeders and gardeners select for characteristics beneficial to humans, nature selects for the benefit of the plant or animal species. Because of the short timespan during which humans have practiced selective breeding, "how poor will be [the] results, compared with those accumulated by Nature during whole geological periods." Since artificial selection has produced the fastest horses, the most succulent fruits, and the most ornate pigeons, Darwin wondered, "What may not natural selection effect?" Unfortunately, by personifying "Nature" as a selective breeder, Darwin confused some readers who wanted to reconcile the new theory with their belief in divine creation.

Evolution became established as fact, not because it prevailed in logical arguments among armchair philosophers or debating teams, but because it unified thousands of disparate observations by comparative anatomists, field naturalists, geologists, paleontologists, botanists, and (later) geneticists and biochemists. That species are related through common ancestry is supported not by one argument or chain of reasoning, but by scores of interlocking research fields, each of which feeds into and supports the rest. Without the overarching concept of a world in the process of change over eons of time, modern science would not exist. The question today is no longer, "Do you believe in Darwin's theory?" but "Do you believe in modern biology?"

If one insists that evolution is merely one interpretation of nature, then what is the alternative? That the thousands of extinct animals—and the species that came before and after them—were not related to one another, appeared full-blown, and had no common connections? Such a model, even if dignified by the label "creation science," cannot lead to fruitful inquiry. It is an answer that prevents any further questions.

Darwin realized that an evolutionary perspective would revolutionize many branches of knowledge, from psychology and paleontology to anatomy and botany. For twenty years he worked on his theory in secret, telling "outsiders" only that he planned to write a "big book" on species and varieties. His friends kept urging him to publish, but he bided his time, gathering more facts, striving for credibility. He was also hesitant to offend religious believers in Scriptural authority—including his own wife. Some historians believe that Darwin's ill health may have been caused, at least in part, by the extreme stress of that inner conflict.

For years he struggled with himself, adding slowly to his "big book" and confiding only in a very few close friends. But then, a young man in a jungle on the other side of the world—a penniless museum collector, tossing in his hammock with malaria—suddenly forced Darwin's hand.

CHAPTER 5 NOTES

p. 51   "Chaos of Delight" *Beagle Diary,* p. 39

p. 51   "The Grand Question . . ." *Notebooks,* p. 228.

p. 51   "answering questions about medicine" Robert Darwin to CD, March 7, 1833, *Correspondence* 1, p. 473.

p. 52   "If we let imagination . . ." Notebook B, July 1837. *Notebooks,* pp. 228–229.

p. 52   "In October 1838 . . ." *Autobiography,* p. 120.

p. 52   "how the birds and beasts . . ." CD to Emma Darwin, April 28, 1858. *Correspondence,* 7, p. 84.

pp. 55–56 "can act on every internal organ . . . What may not natural selection effect . . ." *Origin,* p. 90.

6

SCOOPED BY A RIVAL

Although Charles Darwin became famous for originating biology's great unifying concept—evolution by natural selection—he had to accept a man he barely knew as a full partner in that discovery. "Darwin's theory" is actually the Darwin-*Wallace* Theory; its cocreator was an unknown naturalist, 14 years Darwin's junior, who was working in the rain forests of Malaysia. His name was Alfred Russel Wallace.

An explorer, zoologist, botanist, geologist, and anthropologist, Wallace was a brilliant man in an age of brilliant men. In addition to being cofounder of the natural selection theory, he was the discoverer of thousands of new tropical species, the first European to study apes in the wild, a pioneer in ethnography and zoogeography (study of the distribution of animals), and author of some of the best books on travel and natural history ever written: *Travels on the Amazon* (1853) and *The Malay Archipelago* (1869). Among his many discoveries is "Wallace's Line," a deep channel that forms a natural faunal boundary between the islands of Bali and Lambok in present-day Indonesia. Now known to coincide with an ancient continental shelf, Wallace's Line separates the animals that evolved on the Asian continent from those island species that ultimately derive from Australia. In honor of his contributions to tropical biology, the area between Wallace's Line and the Australian continental shelf is now known to science as "Wallacea."

Born near Usk, a small town on the Welsh border, in 1823, Wallace was raised in genteel poverty. One of his first jobs was helping his brother John survey land parcels for a railroad. While still in his twenties, he served a stint as a schoolmaster in Leicester,

Brilliant naturalist Alfred Russel Wallace independently invented the theory of evolution by natural selection. He was also a biogeographer, popular author, zoologist, explorer, and outspoken social critic. (Author's collection)

where he met young Henry Walter Bates, who shared his passion for natural history and beetle-mania. On weekend bug-collecting jaunts, the working-class would-be adventurers discussed such favorite books as the *Voyage of the H.M.S. Beagle* and dreamed of exploring the lush Amazon rain forests of Darwin's ecstatic descriptions.

Another book also inspired them: Robert Chambers's recently published *Vestiges of the Natural History of Creation,* (1844), the popular but controversial treatise on evolution. Chambers, a literary man with no scientific background, had championed the idea that species had originated through ordinary sexual reproduction, but failed to back it up with solid evidence. Wallace and Bates decided that they would comb the exotic jungles of South America for data that might prove or disprove this "development hypothesis," later known as evolution. When Darwin had embarked on his own voyage of discovery some twenty years earlier, he had had no such clear purpose in mind.

Since naturalists were often dedicated amateurs from wealthy families, Wallace's achievements are all the more remarkable. Unlike Darwin, whose father paid all the expenses of his voyage, even providing a servant, Wallace had to support his expeditions by selling thousands of natural history specimens, mainly insects, for a few cents apiece. When his exploring and collecting days were over, Wallace struggled to support his family on modest author's royalties and by grading examination papers. (He once said intelligence has nothing to do with getting rich, for success at money-getting requires mainly "impudence.")

Bates and Wallace reached Para, at the mouth of the Amazon, in May 1848; they collected specimens and explored the surrounding regions for several months, then decided to split up. Wallace traveled the little-known Rio Negro, leaving Bates to wander in the upper Amazon regions. From 1848 until 1852, Wallace collected, explored, and made numerous discoveries—despite malaria, fatigue, and the most meager supplies.

When he finally returned to rejoin Bates downriver, he found that his beloved 22-year-old brother, Herbert, who had traveled across the world to join the adventure, had just died of yellow fever in Bates's camp. Grief-stricken, exhausted, and still suffering from

Wallace's partner, Henry Walter Bates, is mobbed by curl-crested toucans after shooting one during their expedition to the Amazon. (Author's collection)

malaria, Wallace boarded the next ship for England. With him went his precious notebooks and sketches, an immense collection of preserved insects, birds, and reptiles, and a menagerie of live parrots, monkeys, and other jungle creatures.

In the middle of the North Atlantic, as Wallace suffered a new attack of malaria, the ship burst into flames. He was able to rescue only a few notebooks as he dragged himself into a lifeboat. Everything else burned and sank beneath the waves, he later recalled:

> *I began to think that almost all the reward of my four years of privation and danger was lost . . . How many times, when almost overcome by ague, had I crawled into the forest and been rewarded by some unknown and beautiful species! How many places, which no European foot but my own had trodden, would have been recalled to my memory by the rare birds and insects they had furnished to my collection! . . . And now everything was gone, and I had not one specimen to illustrate the wild scenes I had beheld!*

The measure of Wallace's enormous courage and resilience showed itself shortly after returning to England. With the insurance money he received for part of his lost collections, he immediately set out on a new expedition—this time to the Malay Archipelago (1854–1862).

Wallace studied Malay and several tribal languages, for he was intensely interested (as Darwin never was) in becoming familiar with the manners, customs and modes of thought of non-European peoples. Self-taught in the new science of anthropology, he was a pioneer in recording the customs and languages of the native peoples, and developed a high opinion of their character. He later recalled with satisfaction that while he lived among Dyaks or Malays he never felt the need to carry a gun or lock his cabin door at night.

In Borneo (now part of Indonesia), he tracked orangutans through the deep forest, shot several for the British Museum's collection, and raised an orphaned infant orang in his field camp. Since local tribesmen regarded the red-haired apes as "men of the woods," they were horrified when he shot and skinned them, convinced he would next want to add their own skulls to his collection.

Wallace came to the theory of evolution through his observations of the natural distribution of plants, animals, and human

Wallace's classic, *The Malay Archipelago,* **depicts Dyak hunters capturing an enraged orangutan. Wallace was the first European to observe the red apes.** (Author's collection)

tribal groups and their competition for resources. Like Darwin, he had also been influenced by Thomas Malthus's *Essay On the Principles of Population,* which he had read some years before.

In 1855, while on the island of Sarawak, Wallace composed "my first contribution to the great question of the origin of species." Combining his knowledge of plant and animal distribution with Sir Charles Lyell's writings on "the succession of species in time," he came up with a conclusion about the relationship of living species to fossils found in the same area. His paper *On the Law which has regulated the Introduction of New Species* stated that "Every species has come into existence coincident both in space and time with a pre-existing, closely-allied species." He had been impressed by the distribution of fossils and living animals, the same pattern that had impressed Darwin in South America, when he noted that the ancient giant sloths and armadillos occurred where their relatives still live. Today's species were probably the descendants of similar, extinct forms. This preliminary conclusion, Wallace knew, "clearly pointed to some kind of evolution." ("The how" of evolution, he wrote, "was still a secret only to be penetrated some years later.")

Published in an English natural history journal in September 1855, Wallace's "Sarawak Law" was generally ignored by the scientific world. When he expressed his disappointment to his correspondent Charles Darwin, the senior naturalist replied that Sir Charles Lyell and another good scientist had called his attention to it. What Darwin did *not* say was that his friends were also warning that Wallace might be first to publish an evolution theory unless Darwin raced to finish his own book.

In February 1858, Wallace was living on Ternate, one of the Moluccan Islands, and suffering from sharp, intermittent attacks of fever, which forced him to lie down for several hours every afternoon:

> It was during one of these [malarial] fits, while I was thinking over the possible mode of origin of new species, that somehow my thoughts turned to the "positive checks" to increase among savages and others described . . . in the celebrated Essay on Population by Malthus . . . I had read a dozen years before. These checks—disease, famine, accidents, wars, etc.—are what keep down the population . . . [Then] there

suddenly flashed upon me the idea of the survival of the fittest . . . [that] in every generation the inferior would inevitably be killed off and the superior would remain . . . and considering the amount of individual variation that my experience as a collector had shown me to exist . . . I became convinced that I had at length found the long-sought-for-law of nature that solved the problem of the origin of species . . . on the two succeeding evenings [I] wrote it out carefully in order to send it to Darwin by the next post . . .

If Darwin thought it worthy, Wallace requested he pass it on to his influential friend, Sir Charles Lyell, for publication in a scientific journal. It was this article, *On the Tendency of Varieties to Depart Indefinitely from the Original Type* (1858), that sent Darwin into a panic, fearful that Lyell's warnings about Wallace's being first were about to come true. Darwin had been working in secret for years, confiding his theory to only a few close friends. "Outsiders" (including his sometime correspondent Wallace) knew only that he was writing about the relationship between varieties and species.

Upon receiving Wallace's paper, Darwin was thunderstruck. For years, his mentor Lyell had been urging him to publish the natural selection theory or risk being scooped by someone else. Now, in a panic, he wrote Lyell:

Your words have come true with a vengeance . . . that I should be forestalled . . . So all my originality . . . [is] smashed . . . I never saw a more striking coincidence. If Wallace had my MS sketch written out in 1842, he could not have made a better short abstract [summary]! Even his terms now stand as heads of my chapters.

The crisis could not have come at a worse time. One of Darwin's children had recently died and another was sick with scarlet fever. When he appealed to his friends for advice and help, Lyell and Sir Joseph Hooker arranged to have some of Darwin's early drafts published, along with Wallace's paper, in the Linnaean Society's journal in 1858.

They never considered consulting Wallace. Mail service between England and the Moluccas took several months each way; besides, Darwin, Lyell, and Hooker were prosperous gentleman-scientists, while Wallace was a penurious beetle collector with no social connections. He would have to accept whatever course of action they thought best. So Lyell and Hooker "arranged" the matter to protect their friend Darwin, whom they knew had labored for more than 20 years on the same theory young Wallace had just proposed.

Darwin, usually generous and fair, admitted he was filled with "trumpery feelings," and could not bear to see another naturalist publish "his" theory first. Yet he would rather burn his book, or so he said, than for anyone to believe he stole his ideas from Wallace or behaved in a "paltry spirit." By asking his friends to handle the problem and agreeing to accept whatever resolution they thought proper, he sought to escape the dilemma and any blame for acting improperly.

Since Joseph Hooker was England's leading botanist and Charles Lyell its most eminent geologist, the pair had great influence in scientific circles. In 1858, they persuaded the Linnaean Society of London to publish Darwin's two informal outlines of his views, together with Wallace's essay. Although Wallace's contribution was the only finished paper submitted, the fragmentary Darwin "sketch" (1844) and letter to Asa Gray (1857) were published in first position by Hooker and Lyell. Darwin and Wallace were to share credit as codiscoverers of the theory of evolution by natural selection. In their cover letter accompanying the manuscripts, Lyell and Hooker implied that Wallace and Darwin had agreed to the joint publication. In fact, Wallace knew nothing of this "delicate arrangement" until a year later; he had not even known that Darwin was working on an evolution theory.

Darwin then went furiously to work on *Origin of Species,* completing it in about a year, after almost two decades of putting off the writing. Years later, in his 1876 autobiography, he claimed he had "cared very little whether men attributed most originality to me or Wallace"—a statement that even Darwin's staunchest admirers still find difficult to accept. Wallace was informed of these developments after the fact, and received a copy of Darwin's published book while still in Malaysia. When he returned to England in 1862, Darwin was anxious about Wallace's reactions, and was relieved to discover "how generous and noble was his disposition." Later, Wallace maintained that even if his only contribution was in getting Darwin to write his book, he would be content. But the fact remains that Wallace was not given an opportunity to exercise his nobility or generosity, since the joint publication was decided upon without anyone consulting him.

Wallace modestly stated that his work on the problem was short compared with Darwin's decades of painstaking groundwork and never questioned Darwin's priority. ("I shall always maintain it to be actually yours and yours only.") However, after Darwin's death, Wallace admitted he had "no idea" his paper had thrown the senior naturalist into such a panic.

To the end of his long life, Wallace insisted that being first to publish is meaningless if an idea makes no impact, and that his paper "would never have convinced anybody." In *The Wonderful Century* (1904), he recalled:

> The whole literary and scientific worlds were violently opposed to all such theories . . . [but] the greatness and completeness of Darwin's [book caused] a vast change in educated public opinion . . . Probably so complete a [reversal] on a question of such vast difficulty and complexity, was never before effected in so short a time. [Establishing acceptance of evolution by natural selection] . . . places the name of Darwin on a level with that of Newton.

However one interprets the machinations of Darwin's friends, the "delicate arrangement"—glorified in dozens of books as a classic example of unselfish collaboration—was certainly not one of the brighter episodes in the history of science. But if Wallace could forgive Charles so generously, perhaps so should we.

CHAPTER 6 NOTES

p. 62 "I began to think that . . ." A.R. Wallace, *Travels on the Amazon*, p. 277; Marchant, *ARW Letters*, p. 24.

p. 64 "my first contribution to the great question . . ." A. R. Wallace, *My Life*, 1, p. 354.

p. 64 "clearly pointed to . . . evolution." and "The *how* . . . was still a secret . . ." A. R. Wallace, *My Life*, 1, p. 355.

p. 64 "It was during . . ." ARW, account of 1903, quoted in McKinney, *Wallace and Natural Selection*, pp. 160–161.

p. 65   "Your words have come true." CD to Lyell, June 18, 1858. Francis Darwin, *Life and Letters,* 1, p. 473.

p. 66   "trumpery feelings . . ." CD to Lyell, June 25, 1858. *Correspondence* 7, pp. 117–118

p. 66   "delicate arrangement" is Leonard Huxley's phrase. See A. Brackman, *A Delicate Arrangement,* 1980.

p. 66   "cared very little whether . . ."*Autobiography,* p. 124

p. 66   "how generous and noble . . ."*Autobiography,* p. 121.

p. 67   "I shall always maintain . . ." A. R. Wallace to CD, May 29, 1864, Marchant, *ARW Letters,* p. 131.

p. 67   "The whole literary and scientific worlds . . ." A. R. Wallace, *Wonderful Century,* p. 142.

7

THE ORIGIN OF SPECIES

Darwin had intended to set forth his theory in a big "Species Book" crammed with supporting facts. Dreading the storm of controversy he knew would follow publication, however, he let the data collecting drag on and on. Fifteen years went by, his children grew up, and the book was still mostly unwritten. It was only in 1858, as we have seen, when Alfred Russel Wallace sent him a draft of his own paper on evolution, that Darwin sprang into action. Racing now to publish first, he dashed off the 155,000-word handwritten manuscript in only 13 months and titled it *An Abstract of an Essay on the Origin of Species.* His wise publisher, realizing it was no mere summary of a longer work, cut the first five words.

One of the great classics of science, *On the Origin of Species by Means of Natural Selection, or the Preservation of Favoured Races in the Struggle for Life* was published on November 24, 1859. It is a dense, difficult book, which even Darwin's best friends found rough going. Convinced it would be a commercial failure, he offered to pay his publisher's losses. To his amazement, the entire first printing of 1,250 copies was snapped up by booksellers the first day. It continued selling through six revised editions over the next 17 years and has remained in print ever since.

In the *Origin,* Darwin argued that the best way to account for innumerable facts about living things is by "descent with modification"—or what later came to be known as "evolution." (The word appears nowhere in the first edition; Darwin first used it in his *Descent of Man* (1871), and in the sixth edition of the *Origin* (1872). However, "evolved" is the last word in all editions of the *Origin.*)

ON

THE ORIGIN OF SPECIES

BY MEANS OF NATURAL SELECTION,

OR THE

PRESERVATION OF FAVOURED RACES IN THE STRUGGLE
FOR LIFE.

By CHARLES DARWIN, M.A.,

FELLOW OF THE ROYAL, GEOLOGICAL, LINNÆAN, ETC., SOCIETIES;
AUTHOR OF ' JOURNAL OF RESEARCHES DURING H. M. S. BEAGLE'S VOYAGE
ROUND THE WORLD.'

LONDON:

JOHN MURRAY, ALBEMARLE STREET.

1859.

An intellectual bombshell, Charles Darwin's *Origin of Species* established evolutionary biology and was an immediate success when it was published in 1859. (Courtesy American Museum of Natural History)

Similarities and differences between animal species, Darwin showed, pointed to common origins rather than separate, independent creations. He was not first with that idea. It had been stated before by, among others, the French biologist Jean-Baptiste de Lamarck, Robert Chambers, and his own grandfather Erasmus Darwin. Charles had patiently marshaled the evidence that would convince the scientific world. Having done that, he went on to propose natural selection as the chief mechanism of evolution. Almost from its publication, the *Origin* kindled intense controversies. In the words of Thomas Huxley, "Old ladies of both sexes considered it a decidedly dangerous book."

Previous evolutionary theories depended, in part, on the idea of destinies, set goals toward which organisms must irresistibly strive. Some insisted there must be a mysterious inner drive or vital force pushing each species toward ever greater perfection. Darwin approached living things as natural phenomena, shaped by causes that could be probed by experimental research and systematic observations. For instance, he did not simply theorize that certain plants might have reached far-flung oceanic islands as floating seeds; he soaked many kinds of seeds in barrels of salt water for months, then planted them to see which species would sprout. He did not speculate about the effects of crossing different varieties of domestic pigeons; he performed the breeding experiments. In the *Origin,* he invented a whole new science. And in subsequent books, he showed how to apply it to understanding nature.

Building his case for evolution in a disarming, indirect manner, Darwin brings the readers along almost in spite of himself. The author seems to be reluctantly driven to the idea of natural selection by the evidence, despite every possible objection, which he raises before his critics can. Darwin creates the impression that his theorizing is not especially brilliant or difficult. If anyone had access to the same facts, he implies, they would surely have come to exactly the same conclusions.

Having established evolution as the most plausible unifying principle for many facts of geology, paleontology, comparative anatomy, embryology, and other sciences, Darwin attempted to explain how it works. Natural selection is a two-step process. The

first step is the great variability that occurs in a species population, along with the vast overproduction of eggs, seeds, or
individuals—many more than are needed to insure the species'
survival. On that raw material of individual variation, the second step—selection—can operate. Those individuals with any
slight hereditary advantage over their fellows have a greater
chance to survive and reproduce; the "fittest" traits are passed
on and accumulated by successive generations. "Multiply, vary,
let the strongest live [and reproduce] and the weakest die [leav-
ing few progeny]."

Natural selection soon became popularly known as "survival
of the fittest," but nowhere in the first edition of the *Origin* does
Darwin use that phrase. It was actually coined by the influential
English philosopher Herbert Spencer in his *Principles of Biology*
(1864). Spencer, who was not a naturalist, vaguely referred to
those individuals best able to foster general progress and im-
provement of their society or species. Alfred Russel Wallace,
struck by "the utter inability of many intelligent persons" to
understand what he and Darwin meant by natural selection,
suggested that Darwin substitute Spencer's phrase. However,
when Darwin obliged him by using "survival of the fittest" in
later editions of the *Origin,* readers were still confused; everyone seemed to have his own interpretation of what was meant
by "the fittest."

Still, the phrase caught the public's imagination, and it has been
closely associated with Darwin ever since. Critics said it was a
meaningless tautology—a proposition that simply repeats itself.
Since the "fit" are the individuals that survive, they argued, wasn't
it just another way of saying "survival of the survivors"? That
would mean the theory was "not falsifiable" and therefore unscientific, since survivors always survive.

Aware of that potential pitfall, many evolutionary biologists
have contributed to a useful definition. Fitness, it turns out, is a
relative term. Organisms that are the "fittest" in one environment,
may be completely unsuccessful in another, like the proverbial
fish out of water. Or they may be extremely successful for millions
of years—as the dinosaurs were—only to be suddenly wiped out
by changing conditions.

Alfred Russel Wallace, in his classic *Darwinism* (1889), defined "fitness" from the viewpoint of a naturalist who had spent years observing animals in tropical forests. To Wallace the fittest were "those which are superior in the special qualities on which safety depends":

> At one period of life, or to escape one kind of danger concealment may be necessary; at another time, to escape another danger, swiftness; at another, intelligence or cunning; at another, the power to endure rain or cold or hunger; and those which possess all these faculties in the fullest perfection will generally survive.

They are "the best organised, or the most healthy, or the most active, or the best protected, or the most intelligent, [that will] . . . gain an advantage over those which are inferior in these qualities." Wallace's "fitness" varies with the time of life, or even with the time of day!

During the 1940s, Thomas Huxley's grandson Julian, a shaper of modern evolutionary biology, helped bring the field in line with the new science of population genetics, which developed after Darwin's day. Huxley differentiated between "survival fitness" and "reproductive fitness." Survival fitness concerns the individual's success at growing to maturity, finding food, and living long enough to reproduce. Reproductive fitness concerns efficiency in leaving offspring: such things as clutch or litter size, ratio of males to females in a population, and competitive attractions for the opposite sex. Fitness can also mean the range of variability in a population's gene pool—the bank of available variability it can draw upon—which allows flexibility for change during famines, plagues, or shifts in climate.

In populational terms, fitness simply means reproductive success. The race does not always go to the strong or swift, but to those who manage, by whatever means, to produce the largest number of offspring. Sometimes the "fittest" may be those who attain high social status (and more matings) with bold bluffs or subterfuges rather than physical prowess or strength. Among birds, methods of outcompeting rivals range from displaying colorful plumage to pushing the neighbor's eggs over a cliff.

In addition to establishing the theory of natural selection, *The Origin* was also a founding work on the interpretation of fossils, distribution of plants and animals (biogeography), taxonomy (classification), comparative anatomy, and many other fields of modern biology. However, it skirted the question of human evolution, containing only the single remark that "Light will be thrown on the origin of man and his history." A dozen years later, Darwin tackled the subject of human evolution in his *Descent of Man* (1871).

Origin's facts and theories alone cannot explain the special excitement it generated. According to critic-historian Stanley Hyman, it is also "a work of literature, with the structure of tragic drama and the texture of poetry." It conveys the urgency of a personal testimony, exhorting the reader to discover "grandeur in this view of life." Through Darwin's eyes, we no longer see just a sparrow or a cactus, but a roiling drama of conflict and competition, a dynamic landscape of organic beings caught in a relentless struggle for existence. Nature is "daily and hourly scrutinising, throughout the world, the slightest variations; rejecting [some] . . . preserving [others] . . . silently and insensibly working" to choose and reject, to bestow survival or allow extinction.

"Survival of the fittest" was seized upon by so-called Social Darwinists as a slogan to justify economic and political ruthlessness. "Robber barons" of the Gilded Age—James J. Hall, John D. Rockefeller, Andrew Carnegie—told journalists that their cutthroat business practices were, in the long run, helping society evolve. Elimination of weak and inefficient competitors was the road to progress, with future benefits for all. Darwin himself disavowed such an interpretation. He laughed at a newspaper editorial "showing that I have proved 'might is right' and therefore that Napoleon is right and every cheating tradesman is also right."

Darwin's friend and chief advocate for evolutionary ideas was the zoologist Thomas Henry Huxley. When moralists and politicians tried to offer "survival of the fittest" as their justification for the "naturalness" of ruthless individual competition, Huxley was appalled. The confusion, he pointed out in an 1892 essay, lies "in the unfortunate ambiguity of the term 'fittest' in the formula, 'survival of the fittest.' We commonly use 'fittest' in a good sense, with an understood connotation of 'best' . . . [which we are] apt to take in its ethical sense. But the 'fittest' which survives in the struggle for existence may be, and often is, the ethically worst." Therefore, we should turn our backs on the "law of the jungle" and consciously strive to become a more humane, nurturing, and cooperative species. In the long run, Huxley argued, a kind and compassionate species may be more likely to meet the tests of survival.

Misunderstandings of Darwin's theory were, and are, common. If evolution was really a fact, some critics asked, where are the missing links? In our everyday experience, species seem distinct and not "blurred" as Darwin insisted. One of the most common tests proposed to define species was the impossibility of crosses between them. Although interspecies mating usually cannot produce fertile offspring, Darwin knew that there were many exceptions. Hybrids such as ligers (a cross between a lion and tiger) are not uncommon in zoos, for instance, although it is unlikely that the two species would ever mate in the wild. By 1987, zoologists could point to almost 600 crosses between different species and varieties of mammals that have produced healthy offspring.

Transitional fossils ("links" between major groups) are notably rare because most species remain stable for long periods. When change occurs it is fairly rapid (in relation to geologic time) and often begins among small, isolated populations. Imagine a multilevel parking garage frozen in time. Large "populations" of cars would be found on the various floors, but only a few on the ramps. The time cars spend on the ramps is short compared to time they remain parked, yet each must have traveled the ramp.

In 1861, the discovery of the famous fossil *Archeopteryx* ("ancient wing"), with its feathers, teeth, claws and lizardlike skeleton, provided clear evidence of a transitional form between reptiles and birds. Also, during the late nineteenth and early twentieth centuries, the Karroo region of South Africa yielded a vast gravyard of mammal-like reptiles, a whole array of intermediate species. Among living creatures, there is an unbroken series between lizards and snakes, thrushes and wrens, sharks and skates. Skilled botanists cannot agree on definitions for various species of willow or birch trees, so closely do some varieties overlap.

Other evidence of transitions is found in geographical distribution of living species. On Pacific island chains during the 1930s, for instance, biologists tracked bird populations across thousands of miles, discovering intermediate forms all along the way. Darwin himself was so impressed with a series of such geographic variations in Amazonian butterflies over a vast area, he was moved to remark, "We feel to be as near witnesses, as we can ever hope to be, of the creation of a new species on this earth."

In the *Origin* he pictured evolution as a "Tree of Life" or branching bush, with delicate twigs burgeoning in all directions. Prior to Darwin, natural history was influenced by the ancient idea of the Great Chain of Being, which arranged living things in a linear hierarchy, like a ladder or staircase. Simple, lowly (base) creatures occupied the lower rungs; higher up (nobler) were creatures successively closer to man, the pinnacle of all forms of life. Only angels or other spiritual entities were higher, with God at the very top.

The Chain of Being was a hard mental habit to break. Early evolutionists, such as Lamarck and Erasmus Darwin, transformed the ladder into an escalator. Animals were thought to aspire to the next higher rung, a constant striving upward. Lamarck measured evolutionary "progress" in terms of closeness to man, an appealing idea from the human perspective but hardly fair to the rest of living things. (Old habits die hard; many texts still refer to the "higher primates" or the "manlike apes.")

Darwin realized that "higher or lower," meaning "more or less perfect," was not a scientific way to view the natural world, even though it often crept into his own writing. How could one determine whether a clam is "higher" than a mussel or a hamster "higher" than a field mouse? Each species is the product of a unique history, influenced by habitat, competition, opportunities, and luck of the draw. Galapagos Island finches, for instance, diverged from mainland ancestors to become seed eaters, insect eaters, woodpeckerlike species, and so on. None can be said to be "higher" or "lower"; they have simply adapted to various niches in the environment.

Where the tree of life is very "bushy," representing a dense cluster of many related species, we see a successful group that has radiated into many niches. But if most of the cluster has become extinct, leaving only one surviving species and a few fossils, a common procedure has been to bring back the old evolutionary "ladder." The fossils are then artificially arranged in a direct line, making "progress" or "leading up" to the single surviving twig. This fallacious method fosters the illusion of "finalism"—that species evolve toward a final goal, be it the modern horse or man. A truer view would take into account the twiggy, bushy history of species radiation.

If a group of closely related species survives today, no one dreams of arranging its members in a hierarchy leading to the "highest" one. For instance, there are many species of rodents on Earth and many different antelopes. No one wonders which is the "highest" antelope or rodent. But because only a single twig remains in the case of *Homo sapiens,* we commonly see ourselves as the goal or culmination of all the branches of hominid evolution.

There were, in fact, many species of upright, intelligent primates, most of which died out. We are the only surviving twig of a once-successful cluster that almost became extinct. Yet we imagine the history of our line as if all its branches were striving to become ourselves, the end and summit of evolutionary development. That, in the words of paleontologist Stephen Jay Gould, is "life's little joke."

"With a book as with a fine day," Darwin wrote to Huxley in 1863, "one likes to end with a glorious sunset," as he had done in the *Origin's* concluding paragraph:

> *Thus, from the war of nature, from famine and death, the most exalted object which we are capable of conceiving, namely the production of the higher animals, directly follows. There is grandeur in this view of life, with its several powers, having been originally breathed into a few forms or into one; and that, whilst this planet has gone cycling on according to the fixed law of gravity, from so simple a beginning, endless forms most beautiful and most wonderful have been, and are being evolved.*

Charles had gotten his theory between two covers, and it was a masterpiece. He saw from the start, however, that he needed to convince a group of able, young naturalists to publicly support it. He was well aware that his "unaided book" would not have effected such sweeping changes in science without Huxley's and other partisans' energetic, unrelenting campaign to win acceptance of the new views.

CHAPTER 7 NOTES

p. 71   "Old ladies of both sexes . . ." Thomas Huxley, *Darwiniana, Collected Essays,* II, p. 22.

p. 72   "Multiply, vary . . ." *Origin.* p. 274. 'the utter inability . . ." A. R. Wallace to CD, July 2, 1866. *Letters and Reminiscences,* p. 140.

p. 73   "At one period . . ." A. R. Wallace, *Darwinism,* p. 91.

p. 74   "Light will be thrown . . ." *Origin,* p. 483.

p. 74   "a work of literature . . ." S. Hyman, *Tangled Bank,* p. 26.

p. 74   "daily and hourly scrutinising . . ." *Origin,* p. 93.

p. 74   "showing that . . ." CD to Charles Lyell, May 4, 1860, in Greene, *Death of Adam,* p. 308.

p. 74–75 "unfortunate ambiguity . . . ethically worst" T. H. Huxley, *Coll. Essays,* 9, (Evolution and Ethics), p. 81.

p. 76   "We feel to be . . ." CD, *Collected Papers,* II, p. 92.

p. 77   "life's little joke" S.J. Gould, *Bully for Brontosaurus* (Norton, 1991) p. 168.

p. 77   "With a book as . . ." CD to THH, Feb 26, 1863 *More Letters,* 1, p. 238.

p. 77   "Thus, from the war . . ." *Origin,* p. 484.

8

THE DARWIN GANG: CONVINCING THE WORLD

Darwin was well aware that scientists are not so easily convinced of new ideas. He often complained to his older friend Charles Lyell, who long balked at publicly accepting evolution, that all scientific men should have the grace to die at the age of 60. Then they would not oppose all new doctrines with their inflexible brains, and impede the progress of the next generation. Initially plagued by doubts as he gathered evidence and spun theories, Darwin had first "fixed in my mind three judges, on whose decision I determined mentally to abide": the botanist Joseph Hooker, the zoologist Thomas Huxley, and the geologist Lyell. He would only put aside his "awful misgivings" about publishing the *Origin* if they could agree with his approach and conclusions.

Of the three, only Lyell resisted "going the whole Orang." Privately, he was convinced that Darwin was correct, but in his public statements and writings he refused to come out squarely in favor of evolution. Darwin was annoyed by Lyell's years of fence-sitting and then by his delayed, lukewarm endorsement. Lyell privately admitted that he didn't want to ruffle any of the churchmen's feathers; such calculated diplomacy may have helped him win a knighthood. When Lyell finally embraced the theory in 1868 at the age of 71, he wrote to ask Darwin "if now I might be allowed to live."

Darwin did not conceal his disappointment and wrote Hooker bitterly "the best of the joke is that he thinks he has acted with the courage of a martyr of old."

In addition to his three self-chosen referees, Darwin campaigned to convince about a dozen other top men in natural history of the truth of evolution. He picked and targeted them, keeping running lists of who was still "unconverted." If these colleagues could be won, he thought, his theory would be safe.

In 1844, Darwin had sent an early draft of his book to his trusted friend Hooker, and had put aside money and instructions for his wife, Emma, and cousin Hensleigh Wedgwood to publish it if he should die. Now, a decade later, he had gathered about him a group of friends and correspondents—naturalists, geologists, botanists, zoologists—who would extend his ideas and apply them in various fields. Later he came to rely on them also as his "troops" to do battle in the public arena. Darwin himself shied away from such activity; the thought of public speaking or debate made him physically ill.

First among his "lieutenants," as he called them, was Thomas Henry Huxley (1825–1895), the brilliant and scrappy zoologist who became famous as "Darwin's bulldog." Remembered today mainly as Darwin's combative champion and defending knight, Huxley was a forceful speaker and witty writer who gladly battled to help establish evolutionary biology. He was also the founder of a distinguished intellectual lineage, which includes his grandsons, novelist Aldous Huxley (author of *Brave New World*) and biologist Julian Huxley, the first director general of UNESCO.

Huxley was a first-rate comparative anatomist and paleontologist, as well as an innovative educator who established lab courses in colleges. A tireless campaigner for freedom of thought, Huxley often said he would rather not have students adopt his ideas merely to please him. Critical and independent thought was more important. "It is the customary fate of new truths," he wrote, "to begin as heresies and to end as superstitions."

A schoolmaster's son from a suburb of London, Huxley's boyhood interest in mechanics had been transferred to organisms. He wanted to take them apart and analyze their structures as living machines. As a young physician, at age 20, he discovered a layer of cells in the root-sheath of human hair, which is still known as Huxley's layer.

Thomas Henry Huxley was known as "Darwin's bulldog" because he enjoyed fighting for evolutionary ideas. A zoologist, anatomist, educator, and essayist, he was the grandfather of the novelist Aldous Huxley and biologist Julian Huxley. (Courtesy New York Public Library)

In 1856, Huxley's life was transformed by a meeting with Darwin that won him over to evolution. Darwin's approach to natural history hit him like a revelation. A few years later, upon reading

Origin of Species, he remarked, "How extremely stupid not to have thought of that myself!" Fortunately for Darwin, it was Huxley who was asked to review the book in the influential *Times* of London. His enthusiasm in the 1859 review got the *Origin* off to a promising start, despite harsh critics—including the powerful Richard Owen, zoologist at the British Museum.

The following year, Owen presented a paper at Cambridge declaring that the human brain had a prominent structure that was absent in apes. Huxley publicly stated that Owen was wrong, and that he would soon publish evidence showing that human brains were structurally no different from those of chimpanzees and gorillas. The following year, he kept his word, then expanded the argument into *Zoological Evidence as to Man's Place in Nature* (1863). Huxley's most important book, it showed that muscle for muscle and bone for bone, humans are more similar to apes than apes are to monkeys.

At Oxford University on June 30, 1860, during the week-long meetings of the British Association for the Advancement of Science, Huxley began to earn his nickname of "Darwin's bulldog" by becoming a combative champion of evolution against all comers. In what came to be known as the Oxford Debate, Huxley confronted Samuel Wilberforce, the powerful Bishop of Oxford. Huxley was not a scheduled speaker and had planned to leave the meetings. Robert Chambers, the author of *Vestiges of Creation,* talked him into staying to help defend evolutionary ideas against the churchmen's planned attacks.

Wilberforce was a wily and confident orator. Although he didn't know much science, he had been coached by the jealous Owen and was skillful at sliding around any argument—a talent that had earned him the nickname "Soapy Sam." According to the bishop's version, he got the name because he was always in hot water and always came out of it with clean hands.

Seven hundred men and women, who sniffed an impending battle, crowded into the new University Museum. On the platform, along with young Huxley were Darwin's old teacher, J.S. Henslow, and Bishop Wiberforce, both anti-evolutionists, and his friends Joseph Hooker and John Lubbock, both evolutionists. Non-combattants Dr. John Draper of New York University and Sir Benjamin

Brodie, the Queen's physician and president of the Royal Society, also shared the platform.

Draper droned on for an hour with a mediocre paper discussing Darwin's views, and several clerics and other members of the audience rose to respond. Among them was Admiral FitzRoy, captain of the *Beagle* 30 years earlier, who held a bible over his head and denounced Darwin for having been a viper in his midst. According to Hooker's account, Wilberforce "spouted for full half an hour with inimitable spirit, emptiness and unfairness" without any grasp of the scientific issues, despite Owens's briefing.

Overconfident that the audience was his, Wilberforce turned to Huxley and snidely asked whether he would prefer to be descended from an ape on the side of his grandfather . . . or his grand*mother?* At this, Huxley turned to Brodie, slapped his knee, and whispered "The Lord hath delivered him into mine hands!" The bishop had violated Victorian propriety by attacking his opponent's family, and—worst of all—insulting womanhood!

Huxley waited to be called by the audience, then rose slowly and deliberately. "When we talk of descent," he calmly explained, "we are speaking of thousands of generations, not of one's immediate family." Huxley's speech was never written down, and witnesses have given us several versions of what he said next. It went something like this: "I have listened carefully to My Lord the Bishop's critique of Mr. Darwin's theory, but have not heard him advance any new facts or arguments that have not already been addressed. Except, of course, his question about my own personal predilection in the matter of ancestry. Now, it would not have occurred to me to bring up such a topic. But if the question is put to me: Would I rather have a miserable *ape* for a grandfather? Or a *man* of great gifts and intellect, who uses his exalted position and tremendous influence for the mere purpose of ridiculing those engaged in serious scientific investigations—I unhesitatingly affirm my preference for the ape."

Women fluttered their handkerchiefs while the room rebounded in laughter. Huxley continued with serious, sober arguments, and the young evolutionary biologists Lubbock and Hooker spoke after him. Hooker pointed out that, from the bishop's remarks, it was clear he could never have read Darwin's book and was completely ignorant of botanical science, which had benefited greatly from Darwin's work.

Open resistance had been made to the church's authority over the question of human origins at an influential public forum. Science had demanded its right to pursue investigations touching on the very roots of human nature. Instead of being crushed and ridiculed, Huxley, Hooker, and Lubbock had won a wider interest and fair hearing for the new theories.

Although he claimed that he thereafter treated Wilberforce with perfect courtesy, Huxley could not resist a cruel parting shot at the time of the bishop's death. Many years later, Wilberforce was riding through a field, when he was thrown from a horse and hit his head on a stone. "His end has been all too tragic for his life," Huxley commented. "For once, reality and his brains came into contact and the result was fatal."

To some, scientific investigations of rocks and fossils seemed to undermine faith in Scripture. Churchmen warned that not only unbelief, but even doubt, was dangerously subversive to the social order. Huxley was daring, therefore, when he awarded doubt a high place in the life of the mind; he was pleased to have the same first name as the doubting apostle. To Thomas Huxley, a person's "most sacred act" is to state his or her conviction of what is true. "All the greatest rewards . . . and heaviest penalties of existence cling about that act." He refused to proclaim faith in a belief for which he had no evidence. Accordingly, years later, he coined the term "agnostic," meaning "without knowledge of ultimate reality" to describe his own state of mind, and the term quickly became part of the language. Although he well understood the limitations of mechanistic science—which had no room for spirits, gods, or ghosts—Huxley insisted that its assumptions were the most workable for understanding nature.

When Huxley's firstborn son Noel died, the Reverend Charles Kingsley asked if he was not now sorry he had no religious beliefs. Wouldn't it be comforting to believe that his boy's soul was eternal, and that they might meet again in an afterlife? "My business is to make my aspirations conform to the facts," Huxley wrote, "not to make the facts conform to my aspirations . . . I refuse to believe that the secrets of the universe will be laid open to me on any other terms."

Although Huxley is remembered as the chief spokesman for Darwin's ideas, he had difficulties with some of them. He questioned the sufficiency of natural selection as the main driving force of evolution. Also, he argued with Darwin's insistence that evolutionary change occurred everywhere at a slow, gradual rate. In Huxley's reading of the fossil record, some classes of animals arose relatively suddenly, diverged rapidly, then stabilized unchanged for millions of years. Recent re-examinations of the fossil record have shown that Huxley's original insight was correct, according to an idea that gained acceptance a century later: punctuated equilibrium. According to punctuationalism, many species populations are stable most of the time, changing very little over millennia. Evolutionary change seems to occur first among a very small part of the population, where it proceeds fairly rapidly under certain conditions. Then the genetic change spreads throughout the larger population or replaces it, and the system remains stable for another long period.

Huxley had learned about evolution when he was already a competent scientist. If anyone was the first unofficial "student," raised in Darwinian ideas before 1858, it was John Lubbock, later Lord Avebury (1834–1913). When Lubbock was a boy, his father, a wealthy banker, astronomer, and mathematician, told him that he had wonderful news. Young Lubbock guessed he was going to get a pony to ride. "No, much better than that," John Lubbock senior replied. "Mr. Darwin is coming to live in Down village." "I confess I was much disappointed," Lubbock recalled, "though I came afterwards to see how right he was."

The Lubbocks lived on a grand estate called High Elms in the Kentish countryside, about 3 miles down the road from Darwin's Down House. Young John found in Darwin a teacher, mentor, and father figure who greatly influenced his life and career. From an early age, he became part of Darwin's select inner circle. At the celebrated Oxford Debate, at which Huxley confronted Bishop Wilberforce, Lubbock gave a long, effective defense of evolution using evidence from embryology.

The eldest of 10 children, Lubbock joined the family banking business at 14, then entered politics while simultaneously pursuing a scientific career. While a teenager, he discovered the first fossil musk-ox known from England, thus helping establish the existence of a cold glacial period, which delighted Darwin. His major contributions were in the fields of prehistory and the behavior of social insects.

One of the leaders of what was then known as the "prehistoric movement," Lubbock focused on exploring what had happened thousands of years before written history. To the prehistorians, ancient Greece was just yesterday. They were excited by the stone "hand-axes" and other evidence of early humans collected by the Frenchman Jacques Boucher de Perthes, whose discoveries had met for 25 years with skepticism and disbelief. Lubbock went to France and toured the Somme River gravels in 1860, escorting the English geologist Sir Joseph Prestwich and others to Boucher de Perthes's remarkable stone tool sites. The scientific visitors were impressed by the association of fossil mammoth bones sealed in rock with the stone tools of Ice Age humans. Largely through Lubbock's efforts, Boucher de Perthes's evidence finally became accepted as the basis of a new science, prehistoric archeology.

Lubbock decorated the walls of High Elms with hundreds of ancient tools and weapons alongside his collection from contemporary tribal peoples. He coined the terms for the division between the Old Stone Age and New Stone Age still used today: Paleolithic and Neolithic. In 1865, he published *Prehistoric Times, as Illustrated by Ancient Remains, and the Manners and Customs of Modern Savages,* using comparisons with tribal peoples to reconstruct the evolution of culture, an approach that dominated anthropology for the next hundred years. In 1867, at the urging of Thomas Huxley, Lubbock became the first president of the Royal Anthropological Institute.

As an observer of social insects, Lubbock was on the cutting edge of research. One special room in his mansion contained more than 30 ant nests of many species, and his *Ants, Bees, and Wasps* (1882) summarized hundreds of experiments on their behavior, social organization, and presumed "mental activity." Lubbock was the first to prove that bees have color vision, confirming Darwin's view that flower forms and colors had coevolved with pollinating insects. Nature's glorious flower show was "meant" for insects, and not, as many authors then imagined, to delight humans with their beauty.

Lubbock was elected to Parliament in 1869. He created the first secular bank holiday in England (the last Monday in August, sometimes known as "St. Lubbock's Day") and fought for shorter working hours, the introduction of scientific education into the schools, and the adoption of wildlife conservation laws.

During the 1890's, Lubbock became interested in a group of ancient mounds containing the remains of a great circle of ancient stones. The site, which he considered the finest mega-lithic ruin in Europe—older and much grander than Stonehenge—is near Avebury, in Wiltshire; he promptly bought up the land to preserve it from commercial development. When rewarded for his life of public service with a peerage in 1899, he chose the title Lord Avebury, after the site of his beloved prehistoric mounds.

Along with Lubbock and Huxley, Darwin's close friend and confidante Joseph Hooker (1817–1911) helped establish the idea of evolution in biology. As a young man, Hooker had wanted to be just like Charles Darwin (eight years his senior). He even kept advance proofs of Darwin's *Beagle* journals (obtained by his bota-nist father) under his pillow. Then, like his hero, he half-heartedly pursued a medical career, but left it to sign on as unofficial naturalist on the surveying ship *Erebus.* Among his contributions to the expedition was a remarkable collection of previously un-known plant species from the Antarctic.

Soon after his return to England, Hooker was elated when Darwin sought him out. Within months, he became the great naturalist's closest friend, confidante, defender, and research part-ner—a relationship that was to last almost 40 years.

Their coming together was no accident. Throughout the *Erebus* voyage, long before they knew each other, Darwin had learned of Hooker's adventures and achievements in the same way that Hooker had got hold of proof sheets from Darwin's *Journal:* through the benign meddling of the older generation of naturalists, who passed Hooker's letters from the South Polar Seas on to Charles. Upon Hooker's return, the usually reclusive Darwin sought him out and offered him the task of classifying the *Beagle's* plant specimens, still languishing undescribed in the British Museum. Hooker jumped at the opportunity.

Darwin liked him immediately and admired his vast botanical knowledge. (Hooker's father was the founding director of the Royal Botanic Garden at Kew.) He knew much more than Darwin about plant identification and traditional botany, but Darwin's way of looking at plants was a revelation to him. Unlike professional botanists of the day, Darwin focused on the living plant: its physiology, ecology, distribution, growth, and reproduction.

On January 11, 1844, Darwin revealed to his new friend that he had long been engaged in:

> *a very presumptuous work . . . [most would] say a very foolish one . . . I was so struck with the distribution of the Galapagos organisms . . . I determined to [tackle the problem of] what are species . . . and I am almost convinced (quite contrary to the opinion I started with) that species are not (it is like confessing a murder) immutable . . . I think I have found out (here's presumption!) the simple way by which species become exquisitely adapted to various ends. You will now groan, and think to yourself, "On what a man have I been wasting my time and writing to." I should, five years ago, have thought so.*

With this hesitant, self-satirizing letter, Darwin confided to Hooker the agenda of his life's work, which he had kept secret even from Lyell. Soon after, some fifteen years before publication of the *Origin of Species* (1859), he entrusted Hooker with his preliminary 1844 essay, setting out the theory of natural selection.

Darwin had picked the right man; Hooker was to become his indispensable collaborator and ally in establishing evolution, backing up Darwin's work with pioneering studies of plant distribution throughout the world. In the introduction to his *Flowers of Tasmania* (1857), Hooker became the first respected naturalist publicly to take a stand with Darwin on natural selection, and even dedicated the book to his friend.

Hooker became a frequent visitor at Down House, where Darwin would "pump him" each morning, handing him countless slips of paper asking for specific information on plant classification or distribution. Little by little, they began to piece together the outlines of succession and affinities, which evolved earlier and which later, and how plant families might have dispersed and spread over islands and continents. In the afternoons, they would stroll the sand walk, talking of "foreign lands and seas, old friends, old books, and things far off to both mind and eye."

Before Hooker left on a grand, new expedition to India and Tibet, Darwin loaded him with hypotheses to test, samples to be taken, questions to be answered. Hooker was becoming the world's greatest expert on the distribution of plants, and he shared all his knowledge, research, maps, and specimens with his friend Darwin.

Hooker's three expeditions to India were conducted in the grandest Victorian manner. His massive party included armed guards, bird and animal shooters, cooks, porters, and a crew to collect and press plant specimens for shipment home. Weather was so wet in the Khasia Hills, in what is now Assam, north of Bangladesh, that it took special efforts to dry specimens and press them in papers. He rented "a large and good bungalow, in which three immense coalfires were kept up for drying plants and papers, and fifteen men were always employed from morning till night." His discovery of the rare blue vandan orchid in the Khasias, unfortunately, resulted in an invasion by ruthless commercial collectors who stripped the forests bare of them.

On one expedition to the Sikkim Himalayas in 1848, he traveled by elephant 5,000 feet up a sacred Himalayan mountain, attempting to reach Tibet. But the Rajah of Sikkim, paid by the Chinese to keep Englishmen out of the area, had sent 100 men to capture him. This didn't faze Hooker a bit. He had taken the precaution of hiring his own private security force: 56 Gurkhas, who were "immense fellows, stout and brawny, in scarlet jackets, carrying a kookry [dagger] stuck in the cummerbund and heavy iron sword at their side." By offering to pay both troops not to fight, within two hours he had turned both his and the Rajah's men into a combined army of plant collectors.

Hooker succeeded his father as director of the Royal Botanic Garden at Kew, serving for 20 years (1865–1885), after which time his son-in-law, William Thistleton-Dyer, took over. Although Hooker is best remembered for his contributions to botany, it was he—not Thomas Huxley—who really won the day at the Oxford

Debate with a solid presentation of evidence, *after* Huxley and the bishop had traded barbs. And when Darwin's long hesitation to publish threatened his place in history, it was Hooker (with Lyell) who rescued his claim to fame before the Linnaean Society.

In the end, Sir Joseph Dalton Hooker had gone his youthful daydreams one better—he had become one of Charles Darwin's heroes. In the study at Down House, Darwin hung Hooker's portrait over the mantle next to that of Lyell.

Hooker, Lubbock, Huxley, and six other friends met regularly for dinner on the first Thursday of each month, directly before scientific meetings of the Royal Society. Huxley was the genial ringleader of this extraordinary dining club; most had a strong interest in evolution and were also personal friends of Darwin, who rarely ventured into the city. Since they had no name for the group, which met from 1864 until 1893, they called themselves simply "The X Club." From their informal dinner table, they practically ran British science. Once a year, they held a high-spirited excursion to the countryside, accompanied by their spouses, known as "the weekend for x's and their yv's."

Prominent biologists outside of England found exciting new research directions in evolutionary theory. In Germany, zoologist Ernst Haeckel became known as "the ape professor of Jena" through his widely popular lectures and books, which were translated into dozens of languages. Harvard botanist Asa Gray became America's leading evolutionist, despite disagreements with Darwin about an active role for God in guiding natural selection. In 1876, Hooker came from England to join Gray on an elegant "expedition" to the Colorado Rockies, where the great botanists had a grand time comparing notes and collecting mountain plants.

While his friends and fellow evolutionists often met in London, Darwin remained at his tranquil country estate, where he strolled his woods and conducted botanical work in his greenhouse and garden. Despite regular bouts of weakness, abdominal pain, fatigue, and vomiting, which allowed only a few hours of work a day, he eventually managed to complete thousands of experiments, 17 books and over 100 scientific papers.

Starting on July 3, 1857, two years before publication of the *Origin,* Darwin took on the part-time job of police court magistrate

Darwinian botanists Sir Joseph Dalton Hooker (kneeling, with plant press), director of England's Kew Gardens, and Harvard's Asa Gray (seated next to Hooker) collect plants in the Colorado Rockies in 1876. Their comfortable "expedition" included their wives, an army general, a professional hunter (in buckskins), an angler (with rod), a guide, and camp cook. (Courtesy Michael Huxley)

in the Petty Sessions Court at Bromley, the largest nearby town. His neighbor, banker-scientist Sir John Lubbock (Senior), had talked him into accepting the honorary position. As a magistrate, philanthropist, landowner, husband, and father, who was free of any scandal, Darwin daily demonstrated that one could quietly believe in evolution and "materialistic science" without being a threat to society. He was a gentleman radical, combining innovative ideas with a conservative life-style.

In his oath of office, he agreed to "Keep the Peace of one said Lady the Queen in the said County, to hear and determine divers felonies and also trespasses and other misdemeanours." In the same document, he was also enjoined from doing "anything to upset the religious values of the country." For almost two decades, his name remained on the list of active judges, and he liked to list himself on official forms as Charles Darwin, J.P. (Justice of the Peace).

Even though the part-time position was largely an honorary one, it could sometimes prove an exhausting responsibility. As he wrote Hooker in 1858, "I attended the bench on Monday and was detained in adjudicating some troublesome cases an hour and a half longer than usual, and came home utterly knocked up [exhausted] and cannot rally. I am not worth an old button."

Most of the cases that Darwin adjudicated had to do with domestic squabbles, drunkenness, fights in the local pub, abuse of domestic animals, and, most commonly, violations of the tough antipoaching laws. In Darwin's court during March 1860, for example, a young man was fined for "catching a rabbit [in a wire snare] on his father's plantation." Another case involved a bemedaled soldier charged with assault in a taproom.

One man was charged with "furious driving" of a horse and cart in a public thoroughfare. The driver pleaded guilty to speeding and was fined, his second such offense. A local newspaper's account of the case suggested that if the horse had been allowed to testify, the driver might well have gotten off free:

> The animal was well treated by his master, did not like staying out late, and was anxious to have a good feed in his stall . . . If the little fat beast could have been examined in the matter, [perhaps] he would have . . . taken the blame on himself.

FARNBOROUGH, September 17th.
Present—George Warde Norman, Esq., C. F. Darwin, Esq., W. Waring, Esq., Col. Cator.

Assault at Beckenham—Richard Brooker and John Newell (the latter a Soldier, with three medals), were charged with assaulting James Escott, in the Tap-room of the George Inn, at Beckenham, on the Evening of Saturday the 15th ult. The complainant's face exhibited unmistakable evidence of great violence having been used, and the defendants were fined 10s. each and costs, and the Chairman told Newell that he was sorry to see a soldier, wearing three silver medals, charged with the commission of such an offence.

Furious Driving at Hayes.—Grey Sergeant of Police v. Bennett.—The defendant who resides at Hayes, was charged with having on the 28th of August furiously driven a horse drawing a cart, in the public thoroughfare, to the common danger of the passengers, in the said thoroughfare. To this charge defendant pleaded guilty, and was convicted in 10s. and costs, this was the second conviction for a similar offence. Subsequent information induces us to add that if the little fat beast could have been examined in the matter, he would probably have exonerated his master from the charge of furious driving, and taken the blame on himself; it appears he has a great objection to his master being out late at night, and when an opportunity serves, he starts off at a dangerous speed, regardless of police regulations and all efforts to stop him; he is probably encouraged to do this by the kind treatment he receives on arriving home safe with his master.

PETTY SESSIONS.
FARNBOROUGH, 17th FEBRUARY.

Present—G W. Norman, Esq. (Chairman) F. W Lewin, C. R, Darwin, William Waring, and R. B. Berens, Esqrs.

NIGHT POACHING.—*George Wakeling*, of Bromley, and *Edward Jeffery*, (residence unknown) were brought up in custody of the Police, charged with entering the preserves of Samuel Scott, Esq. of Sundridge Park, on the night of the 16th uit. with a gun, and destroying three Pheasants. From the evidence it appeared that on the night in question, Pickett, the keeper, Ford, his assistant, and a man named Amos Kennard, were on the "look out," and saw the defendants enter Elmstead Wood, very shortly afterwards firing commenced, and carried on until they were interrupted by the keeper and his assistants, when the man ran away and escaped, except Jeffery, who was caught by Ford, between whom a violent scuffle ensued, until Pickett came up to Ford's assistance. In Jeffery's pockets were found the three pheasants and a quantity of large stones, so that no doubt serious mischief was contemplated. Wakeling was subsequently apprehended, and both defendants were convicted and sentenced to three months imprisonment with hard labour, and required at the expiration of the term of their imprisonment, to find sureties by recognizance not to offend again for the space of one year, or in default, to be further imprisoned and kept to hard labour for the space of six months.

MONDAY, JAN. 15.

These sessions were held at Locksbottom, before the following magistrates :—G, W. Norman, Esq. (Chairman), W. Waring, Esq.. C. R. Darwin, Esq., and F. M. Lewin, Esq.

Two women named *Skinner* and *Stevens* pleaded guilty to damaging a fence, the property of Mr. Shepherd, of Cudham, and were each fined 1s. and 5s. costs. The money was paid.

Thomas Wells, of Knockholt, for night poaching on the property of D. Norton, Esq., was sentenced to two months' hard labour, and to find at the expiration of that term sureties for good behaviour for six months, himself in £10 and another in £5.

The case of *George Marks*, who has been summoned by Mr. R. Wilson, the relieving officer of the Bromley Union, for refusing to support his wife, was, in consequence of defendant's ill health, remanded for fourteen days. Mr. C. J. Carttar has been engaged for the defence.

Edwin Mitchell, of Hayes, who was proved to be in company of Jeffery and Wakeling, in Mr Scott's preserves, was charged before R. Boyd and S. Long, Esqrs., at the Magistrates' Clerk's office, on the evidence of Pickett and Ford In his defence Mitchell set up an *alibi*, which he stated his father could prove; but on his being called, he stated that he *thought* his son came home about 12 o'clock on the night in question, but could not speak positively as to the time. Defendant who had left Maidstone Gual only on the previous Friday, for an offence against the Game Laws, was sentenced to the same term of imprisonment as Jeffery and Wakeling.

On the following day (Tuesday), the 18th ult., three men *Patrick McFarland, John Miller*, and *Best Larkin*, were charged before the police sheet with drunkenness, &c., at St. Mary Cray. McFarland, who it appeared was a hawker, and attended before the magistrates with the loss of his coat and hawking licence, on being charged with creating a disturbance, in addition to being drunk, protested that the police were under a mistake, as they knew very well that *all he had done was to take off his coat and offer to fight the best man of the lot*. This mysterious piece of logic was rather perplexing, and occasioned a good deal of laughter in court, but failed to produce a satisfactory result; this defendant and Miller were each fined 5s. and Larkin 7s. and costs, which they paid.

BECKENHAM.—The fatal quarrel of two boys.—We regret to state that the lad, Henry Hollands, who was stabbed on the 10th of January last, by another lad, in the village

Magistrate Charles Darwin served on the local police court, where he dealt with game poachers, brawlers, and speeding drivers, as shown in these cases from *The Bromley Record* newspaper. Reports from several different issues of the 1860s have been combined in this composite page. (Courtesy of the Bromley Library, Bromley, England)

One wonders if the horse's point of view in the court report came from a whimsical, off-the-record remark by Magistrate Darwin, who was well known to have had a special sympathy for horses.

Once he witnessed a man whipping his horse terribly on the road. Pulling to a stop from his own carriage, he angrily told the driver that he was magistrate in the district, and that if the man were seen abusing the animal again, he would haul him into court and throw the book at him.

Darwin would not tolerate any cruelty to animals in his neighborhood. Another time, a gentleman farmer, a neighbor at Down, had neglected some sheep until they died of starvation.

"Though he was ill and weak and it was most painful to attack a near neighbor," William Darwin later recalled, "[my father] collected all the evidence himself . . . and had the case brought before the magistrates, and . . . got the man convicted."

One 1862 case that apparently amused Darwin and the other judges was that of a drunken man, a hawker, accused by the police of being belligerent. He protested that he did not "create a disturbance." "All he had done was to take off his coat and offer to fight the best man of the lot." Apparently, he thought he was being prosecuted for removing his coat. The Bromley newspaper account noted that "this mysterious piece of logic was rather perplexing, and occasioned a good deal of laughter in the court, but failed" to get the man off.

Less amusing were the cases of poaching, which constituted the majority of offenses in the countryside. In one instance, the poachers got into a violent scuffle with a gamekeeper, were sentenced to three months hard labor, and were required on their release to post a year's wages against their future good behavior—or spend another six months in jail. Francis Darwin claimed his father "always seemed to be trying to find an excuse for the prisoner, and usually succeeded." According to one nineteenth-century writer's account, Darwin sympathized with a man who had killed a deer to feed his family, telling the prosecutor: "If tempted in the same way I am sure that I would have done as he has done." Then he fined the man five shillings, and paid the fine himself, instead of sending him to the workhouse for six months. When his fellow magistrates objected that he was promoting disrespect for the law, Darwin waved them off. Displaying a scientist's irreverence for enshrined authority, he pointed out that the law was antiquated, "made a hundred years ago."

Besides, he is reported to have told his fellow magistrates, "I didn't hear much of the evidence, as my mind was full of orchids." At the time, Darwin was raising and experimenting with scores of tropical orchids in his greenhouse, and was equally fascinated by the tough, drab little English varieties that grew wild nearby. They were the subjects of his next major investigation, soon to become famous in his first book published after the *Origin of Species.*

CHAPTER 8 NOTES

p. 79   "fixed in my mind three . . ." quoted in *THH Life and Letters,* p. 166. See also *CD Life and Letters,* ii, p. 197.

p. 79   "if now I might be allowed . . ." Referred to in *Autobiography,* p. 100–101.p. 100

p. 79   "the best of the joke . . ." CD to J. Hooker, *Life and Letters,* iii, p. 9

p. 80   "It is the customary . . ." T.H. Huxley, 1880, in *Coll. Essays,* 2 (Darwiniana), p. 229.

p. 82   "How extremely stupid . . ." *T.H. Life and Letters,* i, p. 170, also *CD Life and Letters,* ii, p. 197.

p. 83   "spouted for full half . . ." J.D. Hooker, quoted in *THH Life and Letters,* 1, p. 183.

p. 83   "The Lord hath . . ." *THH Life and Letters,* i, p. 188.

p. 83   "When we talk of descent . . ." *THH Life and Letters,* 1, pp. 179–189.

p. 84   "His end has been . . ." T. H. Huxley letter to John Tyndall, July 30, 1873, Huxley Papers.

p.84   "most sacred act . . ." T. H. Huxley to Charles Kingsley, Sept. 23, 1860. *THH Life and Letters,* 1, p. 217.

p. 84   "agnostic," T. H. Huxley, *Agnosticism,* 1889.

p. 84   "My business is to make . . ." T. H. Huxley to Charles Kingsley, *THH Life and Letters,* 1, p. 219.

p. 85   "I confess I was much . . ." *Lubbock,* i, p. 15.

p. 88   "a very presumptuous work . . ." CD to J. D. Hooker, January 11, 1844. *Correspondence,* 3, p. 2

p. 89   "foreign lands and seas . . ." J. D. Hooker, *CD Life and Letters,* ii, p. 27.

p. 89   "immense fellows . . ." J. D. Hooker, quoted in Charles Ward, 1827. *Darwin,* p. 260.

p. 92   "Keep the Peace . . ." J. Marsh, Charles Darwin—Justice of the Peace in Bromley, Kent. *Justice of the Peace,* 147 (1983), 636–37.

p. 92   "I attended the bench . . ." CD to J. D. Hooker, December 21, 1858, Correspondence, 7, p. 441.

p. 92   "catching a rabbit . . ." and "The animal was well treated . . . on himself." *Bromley Record,* March 1, 1860, p. 1; *Bromley Record,* October 1, 1860.

p. 94   "Though he was ill . . ." H. Litchfield, ed., *Emma Darwin Letters,* ii, p. 168.

p. 94   "All he had done . . ." *Bromley Record,* March 1, 1862, Petty Sessions, Farnborough for February 17, 1862. Other cases of Magistrate Darwin in *Bromley Record* for February 1, 1860; March 1, 1860; October 1, 1860; January 1, 1862; March 1, 1862.

p. 94   "If tempted . . ." Elbert Hubbard, *Little Journeys,* p. 219.

p. 95   "I didn't hear much..." attributed by Elbert Hubbard, *Little Journeys,* p. 220.

9

ORCHIDS, PEACOCKS, AND APE-MEN

Charles was delighted to see a public craze for orchids sweep England in the mid-1800s, for cultivating them had long been one of his most enjoyable hobbies. Suddenly it seemed that everyone wanted them. Since even professional horticulturalists had no idea how to grow them from seeds, collectors went out to risk tropical fever, snakebite, and hostile Indians to supply the greenhouses of gentlemen and ladies back home. In the midst of this orchid mania, Charles Darwin published *On The Various Contrivances by which Orchids Are Fertilised by Insects* (1862).

His approach revolutionized commonly held ideas about plant sexuality, while breaking new ground for understanding how organisms can influence one another's evolution (coevolution). Previously, naturalists believed that flowers were created to provide beauty, medicines, or perfumes for the benefit of humanity. Inspired by a long-ignored work on pollination, Christian Sprengel's *Nature's Secret Revealed; how flowers and trees bring themselves forth* (1793), Darwin set out to show that flowers were adaptations to accommodate the pollinating insects that evolved along with them. Since flowers from the same orchid plant could not fertilize one another, Darwin demonstrated that "varied . . . contrivances have [as] their main object the fertilisation of the flowers with pollen brought by insects from a distant plant."

Sprengel's idea, that flower parts function to attract insects that aid them in sexual reproduction, was still new and somewhat shocking. Darwin documented case after case in which flowers seemed to have evolved in tandem with particular kinds of insects, in some cases by luring them inside a pollen chamber, in others by providing landing platforms. Following his lead a century later, scientists have discovered even more amazing adaptations. Some orchids give off the sexual smells of female wasps to attract the males, while others even mimic the body shape of the female wasp. Fooled into mating with the flower, the wasp rolls in its pollen, which he will unwittingly carry to another flower.

So convinced was Darwin that the structures of flowers had coevolved with insects that he even predicted the discovery of a bizarre moth that no one believed could exist. The beautiful white Christmas-Star orchids found on the island of Madagascar sport foot-long structures containing nectar only at the bottom. "What can be the use," Darwin wondered, "of a nectary of such dispro-portionate length?" Then, with Sherlock Holmesian logic, he con-cluded that "in Madagascar there must be moths with proboscides capable of extension to a length of between ten and eleven inches! This belief of mine has been ridiculed by some entomologists [scientists who study insects] . . ."

Forty years later, a night-flying moth with a 12-inch coiled tongue was discovered on the island, and the species was named *preadicta*—the moth that was predicted!

What if structures had not evolved for specific adaptations, but were modified or simply shifted to perform different functions? To Darwin, such quirky, "madeover" structures were the clearest evidence of all for evolution:

> *Although an organ may not have been originally formed for some special purpose, if it now serves for this end, we are justified in saying that it is specially adapted for it. On the same principle, if a man were to make a machine for some special purpose, but were to use old wheels, springs, and pulleys, only slightly altered, the whole machine, with all its parts, might be said to be specially contrived for its present purpose. Thus throughout nature almost every part of each living being has probably served in a slightly modified condition for diverse purposes, and has acted in the living machinery of many ancient and distinct specific forms.*

With this approach, Darwin veered away from the concept of "perfect adaptation" by a Designer. Adaptations are not perfect; they are often demonstrably makeshift. It was much more fruitful to focus on the "contrivances" and contraptions, showing the pathways of an organism's specific, unique history.

Darwin would have been delighted by the great strides made in orchid raising during the past 100 years. About 18,000 wild species and 35,000 recorded hybrid crosses are now known. (No artificial hybrids existed until 1856, when horticulturists produced the first "orchaceous mule"—to use the wonderful Victorian term.) Growing orchids from seeds is easy now, since it was discovered some years ago that they will sprout in an agar-sugar mixture. In the wild, the needed sugar is provided by a symbiotic fungus, a fact that was unknown to the Victorians.

Orchid commerce has been recently revolutionized by meristem culture, a type of cloning developed by Frenchman Georges Morel in 1956. By growing bits of apical cells (from the tips of new shoots) in rich nutrients, an indefinite number of "copies" of an orchid can be produced. These plants have not "reproduced" in the normal sense—numbers of identical blooms are really all part of one genetic individual. Although most of us imagine them as tropical exotics, there are plenty of tough, drab little orchids in the cooler climes, including some that grew near Darwin's home in Kent.

By the 1860s, in the wake of the *Origin* and the *Orchid* books, evolution had won over many botanists and zoologists. Many of Darwin's readers eagerly searched for more details about the ancestors of mankind, but Darwin wrote only of plants and animals. However, some of the younger evolutionists had begun to publish pioneering works on human evolution. Thomas Henry Huxley's *Man's Place in Nature* (1863) and the German Ernst Haeckel's *Natural History of Creation* (1866) were among the most influential.

Darwin knew the public was eager to have his own version of human origins from apelike creatures, and with the *Descent of Man* (1871), he finally let the other shoe fall. The time had come, he wrote, to openly acknowledge that "with all his noble qualities . . .god-like intellect [and] exalted powers—Man still bears in his bodily frame the indelible stamp of his lowly origin." Still, he expected that the book would "be denounced by some as highly irreligious."

Darwin took no pleasure in challenging the biblical account of Creation; some scholars believe his guilt and anxiety was one of the reasons he delayed writing the *Origin*. Nevertheless, he insisted that three great "groups of facts" in favor of evolution could no longer be denied: (1) similarities in anatomical structure (and, as we now know, biochemistry) among members of the same plant and animal groups; (2) the geographic distribution of living species, especially isolated islands where species seemed to have diversified from a few common mainland ancestors; and (3) the worldwide geological succession of fossil animals, always in the same layered order in the rocks: invertebrates at the bottom, then fish, then reptiles, then mammals (always the youngest), on top. "It is incredible," Darwin wrote, "that all these facts should speak falsely. He who is not content to look, like a savage, at the phenomena of nature as disconnected, cannot any longer believe that man is the work of a separate act of creation."

Darwin explained that man is not descended from any existing monkey or ape but from ancestors that would be recognizably apelike. They were probably hairy, social animals with pointy ears, and the males may have had large canine teeth, similar to those found today in male gorillas and baboons. He speculated that these "fighting teeth" became reduced in size as the hands, freed from locomotion, evolved along with a larger brain to make stone tools and weapons. That idea, expressed in *Descent of Man,* continued to inspire bitter controversies a century later. As late as the 1960s, a distorted view of primate behavior, based on the dominance of males with large canines, was promoted and widely accepted as the model for early humans. Since then, such newly discovered fossil hominids as "Lucy," however, suggest that human ancestors with small canines were already "handed," and may have walked upright while their brains were even smaller than those of chimpanzees.

The *Descent of Man and Selection in Relation to Sex* (its full title) was actually two books in one. In the first part, Darwin discusses human origins from apelike ancestors, using data drawn from embryology, comparative anatomy, animal behavior, anthropology, and geographic distribution. Aside from a fragmentary Neandertal skullcap, no early hominid fossils were yet known to science.

Darwin also published his famous guess—correct, it now appears—that Africa was the cradle of mankind. He reasoned that it was a center of radiation because both of our closest surviving relatives, chimps and gorillas, still live there. Spurred by a widespread conviction that Darwin had deduced the wrong location for the "cradle of mankind," various fossil hunters have since scoured Europe, Asia, and North America in vain for remains of our earliest ancestors. However, since the 1920s, a growing treasure of early hominid ("manlike") fossils has been found in South and East Africa, and in Ethiopia, evidence that has confirmed Darwin's hypothesis beyond his wildest hopes. Today we know of at least one other species of human (*Homo erectus*) that lived in Asia, Africa, and Europe 500,000 years ago; and of the much smaller-brained australopithecines, who roamed Africa a few million years earlier.

While the first half of *The Descent of Man* is about human origins, the second deals entirely with Darwin's theory of "sexual selection": competition for mates as an important factor in evolution. Why did Darwin combine these two seemingly disparate topics in one work? In his attempt to identify uniquely human adaptations, he became baffled. Certain traits that humans do not share with apes, such as relative hairlessness (more pronounced in women) and musical ability, appear to have no adaptive advantage whatsoever. Then there was the puzzle of human diversity. Adaptation seemed inadequate to explain so many different hair textures, nose shapes, skin colors, and bodily proportions among the world's peoples. Also, he did not think natural selection explained such secondary sex differences as beards on men or elaborate tailfeathers in male peafowl.

Therefore, he took a long look at animal species that evolved traits that were "neutral" or even detrimental in relation to their environments. Peacocks' tails, for instance, only get in the way of feeding or escaping enemies, but they help the cock compete in a different arena: attracting the opposite sex. Similarly, Darwin thought, smoother skin in human females might have evolved to enhance their attractiveness to males. Many other puzzling characteristics, including musical ability, hair texture, or skin pigmentation, might be due to sexual selection.

Darwin sent questionnaires to missionaries and travelers all over the world, requesting information about ideals of beauty among various tribes. He was pleased to find that local standards of attractiveness vary greatly and often are exaggerations of the tribe's special characteristics. To complete his case, Darwin presented these anthropological inquiries alongside a huge compilation of evidence for sexual selection in insects, antelopes, monkeys, birds, and other animals.

Strength or size might be decisive if males competed directly, but in many species they use courtship displays, which (in Darwin's words) "excite or charm" the opposite sex. Female peafowl or birds of paradise select males with the most intense displays of colorful plumage.

Can the reality of sexual selection be demonstrated experimentally? And how might these displays function in evolution? During the 1980s, Swedish ethologist Malte Andersson continued to explore that question. In a memorable field experiment, he showed that female African widow birds do indeed prefer males with exaggerated plumage.

Males of the East African widow bird have 18-inch-long black tail feathers, which they whirl in spectacular displays visible for half a mile. Andersson cut some of the males' ornate feathers short and attached the cut sections to other males' tails. Some were glued right back on their rightful owners, to allow for variables like capture and handling. (This experiment was made possible by the modern miracle of quick-setting superglue.) Results: Males with artificially extended tails attracted four times as many females as those with normal tails or those whose tails were cut short. Within their territories, the number of nests with eggs actually quadrupled.

Still, if elaborate plumage makes the birds more vulnerable to predators, why should evolution favor them, even if females do? Back in 1889, Alfred Russel Wallace suggested that birds with more robust plumage were generally stronger individuals, and perhaps they were really being selected for their vigor, not their beauty. Sexual selection, he thought, was simply a special kind of natural selection, not a different process. Recent studies have followed his lead, exploring the relationship between exaggerated plumage, displays, and good health.

Decades ago, several English researchers proposed that there might be a correlation between a species being prone to blood parasites and males within that species displaying bright colors. In the constant evolutionary war between the birds and infectious protozoa, the healthiest males would have to identify themselves to females in each generation to keep one step ahead of the "bugs" that weakened the population.

In 1987, Andrew Read of the University of Oxford, after an exhaustive study of thousands of species of North American and European songbirds, found such a correlation. Species plagued by much higher levels of parasites tended to be just those species with bright, displaying males—and the males with the brightest plumage tended to have the most resistance to parasites. Female birds may exercise a primitive sense of beauty, as Darwin thought, but selection seems to be working to produce vigor, as Wallace thought. If these new studies are correct, females pick mates who are literally "glowing with health."

One of Darwin's major contributions was that he helped biologists to see species as *populations*. In the older way of thinking, the form of the African lion or the blue whale was considered to be based on a fixed *type* or blueprint that had existed from the beginning, probably in the mind of God. Collectors had wanted "perfect specimens"; variations in color, size, or form were considered bothersome departures from the species ideal. Darwin realized that this ideal type existed only in the minds of scientists, not in nature. He focused instead on the variations, convinced that the range of differences within a population was the raw material of evolutionary change. In modern terms, "survival of the fittest" really means the proportion of genes within a population that is passed on to succeeding generations. The real battle is not over how much food or territory an individual can grab in a lifetime, but over which characteristics make certain individuals more successful in leaving descendants that resemble themselves.

Darwin was also a pioneer in gathering facts that might lead to understanding the evolution of behavior as well as structure. At a time when most evolutionists were dissecting dead specimens and comparing muscles and bones, he published the first modern book

Signals of fear, aggression, submission, and pleasure among animals, along with the possible evolution of these behaviors, were the subject of Darwin's book on *Expression of the Emotions,* a foundation for modern animal behavior studies. (Author's collection)

on behavioral evolution, *The Expression of the Emotions in Man and Animals* (1872).

Among his many contributions to this field, Darwin identified certain behaviors that were later called "fixed action patterns": a species' particular way of courting, fighting, resting, or feeding. He mentions, for instance, how dogs may turn circles and scratch the ground before going to sleep on a carpet, "as if they intended to trample down the grass and scoop out a hollow, as no doubt their wild parents did." He credits his grandfather Erasmus as the first naturalist to describe such repeated, instinctive animal behaviors which later occupied the attention of hundreds of researchers.

Darwin also wrote to many travelers and missionaries about the facial expressions of peoples in the far-flung corners of the planet. How did an Australian tribesman or an Andaman Islander show grief, surprise, or anger? Somewhat to his own surprise, he found that the same state of mind is expressed throughout the world with remarkable uniformity.

But the main thrust of *Expression of the Emotions* was to carry the evolutionary argument a step farther than he had before. Comparing the behaviors of animals, Darwin attempted to show that signals of threat or submission, joy, and even guilt, are not unique to humans. Spoken language had been added onto ancient communication systems that used sounds, postures, and gestures. Our smiles, for instance, had evolved from the monkey's grimaces of submission. In knocking down the wall between human and animal behavior he was challenging future generations to understand how human behavior had emerged in an unbroken continuity from the animal world. And he was following the grand view he had written in a notebook years earlier: "We may all be netted together."

CHAPTER 9 NOTES

p. 97   "varied contrivances . . ." *Orchids,* p. 1
p. 98   "What can be the use . . ." *Orchids,* p. 63
p. 98   "Although an organ . . ." *Orchids,* p. 283.
p. 99   "with all his noble . . ." *Descent of Man,* ii, p. 405.
p. 99   "be denounced by some . . ." *Descent of Man,* ii, p. 395.
p. 100   "It is incredible that . . ." *Descent of Man,* ii, p. 386.
p. 102   "excite or charm," *Descent of Man,* ii, p. 398.

p. 105   "as if they intended . . ." *Expression of Emotions,* p. 42.

p. 105   "We may all be netted . . ." Notebook B, July, 1837. *Notebooks,* pp. 228–229.

10
GHOSTBUSTERS: NATURALISTS AND THE SUPERNATURAL

Humanity's newfound kinship with the apes disturbed many people's cherished beliefs. Even Benjamin Disraeli, the British Prime Minister, asked in a famous 1864 speech: "Is man an ape or an angel?" If that was the question, said Disraeli, then he was "on the side of the angels."

Darwin offered little comfort, however, to those who sought to replace religion with scientific authority. While the church might claim absolute certainty, he maintained that scientific truth was a matter of probability. In 1861, he wrote a friend that "the change of species cannot be directly proved," and admitted he could not account for why some species have evolved and others have not. The theory "must sink or swim according as it *groups and explains [disparate] phenomena.* It is really curious how few judge it in this way, which is clearly the right way."

Why would Darwin expect any thinking person to accept a theory that could not directly be proved? Because it was productive; it worked. Applying it produced a torrent of discoveries, insights, and new information. Connections arose between formerly scattered disciplines: comparative psychology, geology, botany, zoology, anatomy, paleontology. Working scientists found that thousands of formerly isolated facts began to make sense within the larger picture of evolution. Darwin's insistence that we all have to live with uncertainty was as unsettling in his time as the notion that we are descended from apes.

Traditional religion was in crisis. Some churchmen attacked all scientists—particularly evolutionists—as "materialists" who would destroy society by undermining the belief in immortal souls and an afterlife. By "materialism" they were not referring to a fondness for wealth and possessions. Darwin and other scientists focused on the properties of *matter,* analyzing what could be seen or measured, and leaving gods, spirits, and miracles out of their theories. In 1864, eleven thousand Anglican clergymen signed a declaration at Oxford that the Bible and its miracles must be accepted as true history. A decade later, in an address at Belfast, the physicist John Tyndall gave a "materialist's" reply. While you are not urged to erect science into an idol, he told his audience, we scientists claim unrestricted right of search. Tyndall concluded that the church's long monopoly on questions of human origins and nature was at an end and that all biology was now founded on evolutionary theory.

Despite their basic agreement on evolution, Darwin and Wallace held opposing views about nature and the supernatural. Darwin sought the "laws" or regularities in natural processes, and refused to speculate on any grand cosmic plan or purpose. Such questions, he thought, were beyond the realm of science: "A dog might as well speculate on the mind of Newton. Let each man hope and believe what he can." Wallace was a maverick, a rebel within "materialist" science. While he was no supporter of orthodox religion, Wallace became convinced that the human intellect could only have evolved with assistance from unknown, supernatural forces. And he felt—unlike Darwin—that spiritual forces could be the subjects of scientific investigation.

Oddly enough, he was even stricter than Darwin in applying natural selection to his research on insect coloration or bird courtship. But Wallace was stymied on the question of the human brain. Since Darwin had stressed that natural selection makes an organism only as complex as survival demands, Wallace wondered how ape-men could have acquired "an instrument . . . developed in advance of the needs of its possessor."

Early humans would have needed only a gorilla's intelligence to survive. Yet the tribal peoples Wallace encountered on his travels seemed every bit as intelligent as "civilized" folk, despite their

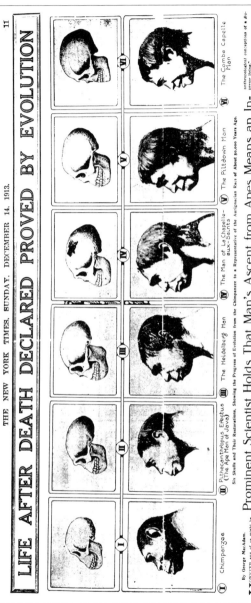

Combining science and religion, Spiritualists claimed in 1913 that fossils of early humans "proved" that spiritual evolution had taken place. Most scientists disagreed, but the *New York Times* gave these views respectful coverage. Piltdown Man was later found to be a hoax. (Courtesy American Museum of Natural History)

primitive technologies. Why had humans everywhere evolved brains capable not merely of speech but also (when educated) of composing symphonies and doing mathematics? While our bodies had been shaped by natural selection, he concluded, some supernatural power must have intervened to expand the human mind.

When Wallace first published this solution to the "brain problem" in 1864, Darwin wrote him: "I differ grievously from you; I can see no necessity for calling in an additional and proximate cause [i.e., a supernatural force] in regard to man . . . I hope you have not murdered too completely your own and my child"— meaning the theory of natural selection. In Darwin's view, natural selection was sufficient to account for the emergence of the human mind, given slow, gradual evolution. Wallace continued to be plagued by the problem. In one of his later books, published years after Darwin's death, Wallace wrote that *Homo sapiens* has "something which he has not derived from his animal progenitors—a spiritual essence or nature, capable of progressive development through conscious internal struggle." The evolution of this special human quality "could only find explanation in the unseen universe of spirit."

Since Wallace's time, with the discovery of fossil man-like creatures from Africa dating back almost four million years, we have additional evidence to ponder. Early upright-walking hominids known as australopithecines have been found with braincases a third the size of our own. Later, they were followed by the larger-bodied *Homo erectus,* with brains half as big as ours. Darwin and Wallace, it now appears, were right about a gradual, progressive expansion of the brain. Nevertheless, the evolution of its workings is still a mystery. Paleontologist Stephen Jay Gould suggests that many "higher" functions of the brain may have come along with complex social behavior, specifically including language. According to Gould's analogy, if you design a computer to handle business accounting, its very structure may also be capable of word processing or working out musical harmonies. They would be side effects of its basic design for other functions.

Wallace eventually became convinced that the world was made for mankind—that all of plant and animal evolution was designed by a supernatural intelligence to prepare the planet for human needs. Adopting this view of a preordained plan for nature, with mankind at its center, cost him a good bit of his scientific reputation. In 1903, Wallace published *Man's Place in the Universe,* in which he marshaled evidence for his view that all of prior evolution on Earth was a preparation for humans. Although he denied it, many thought Wallace was trying to revive traditional religious explanations of divine plan and purpose, clothed in the language of science.

American humorist Mark Twain found Wallace's book an irresistible target for satire. In his spoof on Wallace, "Was the World Made for Man?" (1904), Twain wrote "it was foreseen that man would have to have the oyster" to eat. However, a whole slew of oyster ancestors had to come first, because "you cannot make an oyster out of whole cloth." After millions of years, when the oyster was finally evolved, it started to think about how it got there. "An oyster has hardly any more reasoning power than a scientist has, and so . . . this one jumped to the conclusion that the nineteen million years was a preparation for *him;* but that would be just like an oyster, the most conceited animal there is, except man."

Wallace came to his belief in "a universe of spirit" gradually, over many years. He had been impressed by experiments with hypnotism while still a young man, and had been fascinated by "abnormal states of mind" in Amazonian Indian rituals. In Indonesia, he watched people commonly fall into trances, become "possessed," and speak with their dead relatives. (Darwin, by contrast, had never made any real attempts to understand tribal languages or religion during his travels around the world.) Eventually, as Spiritualism developed into a major popular movement in nineteenth century England and America, Wallace became one of its major spokesmen.

Spiritualism was a reinterpretation of ancient Eastern beliefs, mixed with the Western desire to "secularize" the soul and establish its existence "scientifically." Although a tradition of ghosts and spirits has always persisted on the fringes of Western culture, the modern movement began in 1848 with Margaret and Kate Fox, sisters born into a poor family in upstate New York. When the Fox sisters put questions to "spirits," they received loud rapping noises in response. Their fame spread, and soon many other "mediums"

A SPIRIT-RAPPING SÉANCE!

A SPIRIT DRAWING. BY OUR OWN MEDIUM.

The Spiritualist fad was satirized by Victorian cartoonists. Skeptics characterized sitters' enthusiastic testimony about the marvels that seemed to defy the laws of nature as "what foxes will say, geese and asses believe." (Courtesy New York Public Library) arose. (Thirty years later, after gaining fame and fortune, one of the sisters admitted that she had produced the taps by snapping her big toe inside her shoe.)

Spiritualist activities in England and America enjoyed tremendous popularity and attracted people with a wide spectrum of beliefs. Some were sincere seekers like Wallace, others were convinced they had "psychic gifts," and a few were cynical fakers who grew rich preying on believers. Many gatherings, called seances, were held in private homes, where mediums claimed to communicate with the spirit world. But newspapers lampooned the mediums' proceedings with cartoons captioned "what foxes will say, geese and asses will believe."

As public interest grew, many other "mediums" arose and some became wealthy celebrities, comparable to pop stars. Among the more famous were Daniel Dunglass Home, Dr. Henry Slade, Frank Herne, and Charles Williams. All invited prominent scientists to come to their seances, which were usually held in darkened rooms. There the mediums produced such wonders as "automatic writing," musical instruments that played by themselves, floating tables, glowing spirit hands, and the visitations of spirit beings.

Darwin's cousin and brother-in-law Hensleigh Wedgwood had told him of ghostly accordions that played by themselves and of tables mysteriously rising off the floor. He had begged Charles to come witness these "experiments" that bridged the gap between Emma Darwin's belief in an afterlife and Charles's "materialist" science.

Charles, now in his mid-sixties, made the excuses that he was "too tired," "too busy," or "too ill" to accept Hensleigh's constant invitations. He told his family that seances were "wicked and scandalous proceedings." Charles and Emma had never ceased mourning their two children who had died, particularly Annie, the 10-year-old who succumbed at Easter, 1851. Anyone who preyed on the grief of bereaved relatives was, to Darwin, beneath contempt.

Henrietta Darwin recalled that in January 1874, at the home of her uncle Erasmus, "a seance was arranged with Mr. Williams, a paid medium, to conduct it." Charles, who had not actually been present for the fireworks, wrote that Williams "made the chairs, a flute, a bell, and candlestick and fiery points jump about in my

brother's dining-room, in a manner that astounded every one."
Charles retired to lie down "before all these astounding miracles,
or jugglery, took place," commenting "the Lord have mercy on us
all, if we have to believe in such rubbish."

A few days later, Darwin practically ordered Professor Huxley,
despite protests that he was busy, to attend "a smaller and more
carefully organized" seance at Hensleigh Wedgwood's home.
Darwin's son George, then aged 29, attended with Huxley (incog-
nito, as "Mr. Henry," his middle name), and both wrote reports of
what they saw and heard. Though bottles moved around and a
guitar played by itself, they concluded they had observed nothing
but crude trickery. As Darwin had hoped, his son learned a lesson
about science, belief, and evidence he would never forget. "Unless
I had seen it," George wrote, "I could not have believed in the
evidence of . . . my uncle, being so worthless." Darwin even wrote
to a newspaper, urging a journalist to expose Williams "who has
imposed on the public for so many years."

**Floating chairs, self-playing musical instruments, and mysterious voices
appeared at Victorian seances, convincing many sincere observers that a
"medium" had put them in touch with the spirits of departed souls.** (Author's
collection)

In 1876, one of the most popular mediums in London was the newly arrived American Henry Slade, who was known as the "slate-writing medium." Slade's specialty was posing questions to the spirit of his dead wife and receiving mysteriously written answers on slates. Young Edwin Ray Lankester, an evolutionary biologist who had been Thomas Henry Huxley's student, paid to attend a seance at Slade's with hope of catching him in trickery. Boldly, he snatched the slate from the medium's hand in the darkened room and found an answer written on it before he had finished asking his question. Lankester hauled Slade into police court as a "common rogue"—the first time a scientist had ever prosecuted a psychic for conducting fraudulent "experiments." In a letter to the *Times* of London, he publicly denounced the "astounding credulity" of certain scientists, and singled out Wallace for allowing discussions of Spiritualism at a recent scientific meeting.

Alfred Russel Wallace gladly offered to appear as star witness for Slade's defense. A frequent patron of mediums, Wallace sincerely believed there had been no trickery behind the extraordinary "phenomena" he and others had witnessed at Slade's. Wallace was respected as an author, naturalist, and explorer, the discoverer of scores of new species, a pioneer in zoogeography, and coinventor of the theory of evolution by natural selection. But he constantly courted ruin by championing such unpopular causes as socialism, pacifism, wilderness conservation, women's rights, psychic research, and Spiritualism. He had even written an influential book entitled *Miracles and Modern Spiritualism.* It was easier for him to accept miracles than the idea that a trusted acquaintance would lie to him.

Darwin, on the contrary, was convinced that all "spirit-mediums" were "clever rogues," preying upon the credulous and bereaved. He wrote Lankester that he considered it a "public benefit" to put Slade out of business, and quietly contributed funds to the cost of prosecution.

The judge at Slade's trial said he understood that Spiritualism was "a kind of new religion" and did not wish to offend sincere believers. But the question before the court was: "Did these people fraudulently represent as an act of spiritual agency certain things

Messrs. SLADE and LANCASTER,

In a Scene from the New Farce, "The Happy Medium; or, No Spirits should be above Proof."

Depicted in this 1876 magazine caricature are biologist Ray Lankester ("Lancaster") and spirit-medium Henry Slade, adversaries in a bizarre courtroom drama. Charles Darwin sided with Lankester, Alfred Russel Wallace with Slade. (Courtesy of Society for Psychical Research) which were done by themselves?" Concluding that he "must decide according to the well-known course of nature," the judge sentenced Slade to three months' hard labor in the House of Corrections. Slade later wriggled out on appeal and never served his sentence. Nevertheless, Darwin was delighted with the verdict and wrote Lankester an effusive letter of congratulations.

Three years after the trial, in 1879, Darwin tried to drum up support for a government pension for Wallace, who was always in dire financial straits. But when Darwin wrote to his botanist friend Sir Joseph Hooker, who had good friends on government committees, Hooker refused to help. "Wallace has lost caste terribly," he replied, "not only for his adhesion to Spiritualism, but by the fact of his having deliberately and against the whole voice of the committee" allowed the paper on "thought transference" to be read at the scientific meetings.

Undaunted, Darwin replied that Wallace's beliefs were "not worse than the prevailing superstitions of the country"—meaning

Hensleigh Wedgwood, left, tried to convince his brother-in-law Charles Darwin that he had seen ghosts at seances. Celebrated "medium" Henry Slade, right, claimed to produce "spirit-writing" on slates. (Both courtesy New York Public Library)

organized religion. Darwin and Huxley twisted a few more arms, then personally wrote to Prime Minister Gladstone, who passed the petition on to Queen Victoria. In the end, Wallace got his modest pension and was able to continue writing a fruitful series of articles and books.

Unlike Darwin, Thomas Huxley treated the Spiritualists' claims with a good deal of humor. True to form, he outfoxed them at their own tricks. Having learned that the Spiritualist movement started with two teenage girls who produced phony "spirit raps" with their feet, Huxley became adept at loudly snapping his second toe inside his boots. Psychics were confounded, and true believers astounded. "To produce the best effect," he wrote, "it is advisable to have thin socks and . . . to pick out a thin place in the carpet, so as to profit by the resonance of the floor."

But Huxley did not fault Wallace's observational powers at seances because it is "much more difficult to make such observations and interpretations in a room full of people, stirred by the expectation of the marvelous . . . than in the solitude of a tropical forest . . . A man may be an excellent naturalist or chemist; and yet make a very poor detective." Huxley even had a kind word for well-performed hoaxes. "Fraud is often genius out of place," he once remarked. "When it is well performed, I confess . . . a certain sneaking admiration."

For several years after the Slade trial, Hensleigh Wedgwood and Darwin did not see each other, so hopelessly were they estranged by the Spiritualism controversy. In 1880, however, Hensleigh sent him a long handwritten manuscript: the great synthesis, he thought, of science and religion. Would Darwin read it and perhaps suggest where it might be published?

In a melancholy mood, Darwin may have remembered the time young Hensleigh had gone to bat for him in the matter of the *Beagle* voyage so many years before. To Hensleigh, too, he had once been willing to entrust his natural selection theory were he to die prematurely. But these old friends, who had once been so close, were now hopelessly estranged over the question of science and the supernatural. The four years since they had last visited seemed like forty.

"My dear Cousin," Darwin wrote, "It is indeed a long time since we met, and I suppose if we now did so we should not know one

Darwin's ghostbuster, Professor Ray Lankester, holds up the slate on which the professional "medium" Henry Slade (left) caused mysterious messages to appear. His prosecution of Slade in 1876 was the first time a scientist had charged a psychic with criminal fraud. (American Society for Psychical Research)

another; but your former image is perfectly clear to me." Sadly, he refused even to read Hensleigh's paper, commenting that "no reputable scientific journal would publish it." More than a century later, it remains among Darwin's personal papers, still unpublished.

Hensleigh's wish to reconcile biblical creation with natural science was hardly original; many others had tried it. Three centuries earlier, philosopher Sir Francis Bacon had spoken of Two Books: the book of God's works (nature) and the book of God's words (the Bible). Bacon believed that both books would lead to truth; whatever the human mind could discover about the workings of nature must eventually harmonize with Scripture. Darwin had even quoted Bacon's "Two Books" opposite the title page of *Origin of Species* as a hopeful banner of conciliation.

Scriptural geologists were trying hard to make the torrent of new fossil discoveries square with the Book of Genesis—but they were failing. A very different story about the history of life on Earth was revealed by the record of the rocks. Some fundamentalist Christians condemned evolutionary biology as "Satanic," while religious "flat-earthers" even resisted the idea that Earth is a globe. In America, religious groups repeatedly tried to ban the teaching of evolution in the public schools. In a famous court case in 1925, a science teacher named John T. Scopes was convicted of breaking a church-sponsored state law against teaching evolution in Dayton, Tennessee. The Scopes trial attracted international attention, and the law was eventually repealed as unconstitutional. During the 1970s, Arkansas fundamentalists succeeded in enacting a new state law requiring "equal time" in biology classrooms for their own brand of science—"creation science." In 1981, a lawsuit brought by the American Civil Liberties Union overturned that statute, too. The judge ruled that "creation science" was not science at all, but an attempt to impose sectarian religion on the teaching of biology.

Science and religion were not always at war, however. Many of the same learned men who were shaping biology were conservatively religious, and many naturalists were churchmen. Father Gregor Mendel, for instance, founded the science of genetics in a monastery garden. Some churches attempted to incorporate evolution into their teachings, and interpreted the "seven days" of creation in terms of millions of years. Like Wallace, they saw evolution as part of a divine plan, guided by occasional spiritual or supernatural intervention.

Who can blame the Victorians for wanting the best of both worlds? Many of them believed and hoped that science would soon prove the truth of religion—which made them easy prey for con-men who claimed to contact "spirits." While many people welcomed new scientific discoveries, they also cherished the traditional beliefs that gave them comfort and hope. During the 1950s, a popular play called *Inherit the Wind*, based on the Scopes trial, explored the sometimes painful trauma of accepting new knowledge. The play's defending lawyer, based on the real-life Clarence Darrow, tells the jury he understands that a major change in ideas can be painful, especially when it threatens longstanding beliefs:

> *Progress has never been a bargain. You've got to pay for it. Sometimes I think there's a man behind a counter who says, "All right, you can have a telephone, but you'll have to give up privacy, the charm of distance . . . Mister, you may conquer the air but the birds will lose their wonder and the clouds will smell of gasoline!"*

CHAPTER 10 NOTES

p. 107   "Is man an . . ." *LondonTimes* November 26, 1864.
p. 107   "the change of species . . ." CD to J. Hooker, April 22, 1861, F. Darwin, *CD Life and Letters,* 2, p. 362.
p. 108   "A dog might . . ." CD to Asa Gray, May 22, 1860. *Life and Letters,* ii, p. 312.
p. 108   "an instrument . . ." A.R. Wallace, 1869, quoted in *More Letters,* 2, p. 40.
p. 110   "I differ grievously . . ." CD to A.R. Wallace, March 27, 1869 *More Letters,* 2, p. 39.
p. 110   "something which . . ." A. R. Wallace. *Darwinism,* 1889, p. 478.
p. 111   ". . . it was forseen . . ." Mark Twain, "Was the World Made for Man?" (circa 1904) *Letters From the Earth,* p. 167.

p. 115   "public benefit," E.R. Lankester, *Warner Library of Literature,* p. 4391.

pp. 115, 117 "Did these people . . ." Judge Flowers, London *Times.* 1876.

p. 117   "Wallace has lost caste . . ." J. Hooker to CD December 18, 1879. Unpublished letter, Darwin Manuscript Library. "not worse than . . ." CD to T.H. Huxley, Nov. 1880. Huxley Papers, Imperial College archives. Cited in R. Colp, "I Will Gladly Do My Best," *Isis* 1992, 83, P. 15.

p. 118   "To produce the best . . . floor." and "much more difficult . . . sneaking admiration." T. H. Huxley, *Pall Mall Gazette,* January 1, 1889, pp. 1–2.

pp. 118, 120 "My dear Cousin . . ." CD to H. Wedgwood. May 5, 1880. Unpublished letter, Darwin Library.

11

THE TANGLED BANK

One of the secrets of Charles Darwin's greatness was his pleasure and wonder in the small, commonplace features of the Earth that most of us ignore. While his wealthy neighbors in the English countryside amused themselves with lawn parties and cricket matches, Darwin loved strolling his woods and fields, lifting rocks and poking logs, exercising his "enlarged curiosity" as he had done since childhood. To the end of his life, he never tired of watching the bees in his kitchen garden, the insect-eating plants in his greenhouse, and the earthworms in his fields.

The final paragraph of *Origin of Species* contains Darwin's image of a "tangled bank," his metaphor for nature itself:

> *It is interesting to contemplate a tangled bank, clothed with many plants of many kinds, with birds singing in the bushes, with various insects flitting about, and with worms crawling through the damp earth, and to reflect that these elaborately constructed forms, so different from each other, and dependent upon each other in so complex a manner, have all been produced by laws acting around us.*

Darwin saw a web of interrelationships binding the various plants and animals into a community. (The word "ecology" was invented by his German disciple Ernst Haeckel, in 1866.) Not only is the bank's vegetation entangled; but the lives of its various creatures are also intertwined. Evolution is more than change within individual species; it builds up intricate, intertwined relationships between the Earth and its inhabitants.

In the metaphor of entanglement, Darwin mentioned the organisms he would later study in detail, devoting whole books to common plants and earthworms. He worked out methods for untangling his beloved Tangled Bank; underlying its surface confusion were regularities and relationships. And he promised to untangle them not in far-off rain forests or exotic wilderness, but in the English countryside. There was wonder enough in a familiar and commonplace habitat—like the banks of the River Severn he had played upon as a child.

Millions of years of evolution produced its community of life, no less than the more exotic "inhabitants of South America" with which he begins the *Origin of Species.* What was learned among strange creatures in far-off lands he brought back home. Natural selection and adaptation could be observed in one's own country garden, which—for more than forty years after returning from his global voyage—is exactly what Darwin did.

Insectivorous Plants (1875), Darwin's 14th book, began with some "idling" observations he made while strolling the countryside for recreation:

> *During the summer of 1860, I was surprised by finding how large a number of insects were caught by the leaves of the common sun-dew* (Drosera rotundifolia) *on a heath in Sussex. I had heard that insects were thus caught, but knew nothing further on the subject. I gathered by chance a dozen plants, bearing fifty-six fully expanded leaves, and on thirty-one of these dead insects or remnants of them adhered . . .*

He decided to study Venus's-flytraps, sundews, and pitcher plants, and eventually established as fact that they are actually meat-eaters. Not long after publishing the *Origin,* he had developed a special affinity, even an affection, for carnivorous plants. When American botanist Asa Gray suggested he might better occupy his time, Darwin wrote: "Depend on it you are unjust on the merits of my beloved *Drosera* [the sundew]; it is a wonderful plant, or rather a most sagacious animal. I will stick up for *Drosera* to the day of my death." Venus's-flytraps, with their hinged, spiked leaves that snap closed on insect victims, Darwin thought "the most wonderful plant in the world." His wife, Emma, wrote to Lady Lyell: "He is treating *Drosera* just like a living creature, and I suppose he hopes to end in proving it to be an animal."

Emma was not exaggerating. In addition to Darwin's stated aim of reconstructing the steps between the flytrap and ordinary plants, he also seems to have had hopes of bridging the plant-ani-

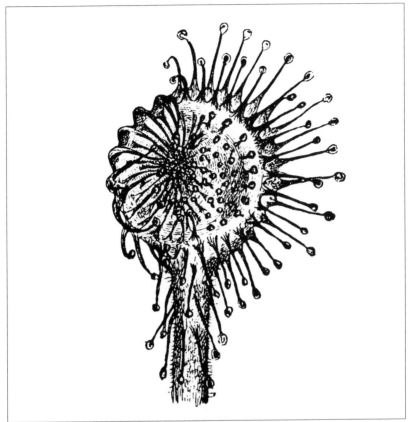

Round-leafed sundew plant (*Drosera*) closes its tentacles over a bit of meat, as illustrated in Darwin's book *Insectivorous Plants*. (Author's collection)

mal gap. "By Jove," he wrote to his friend Joseph Hooker, "I sometimes think *Drosera* is a disguised animal."

Darwin also studied the power of movement of the plants when capturing prey, the secretions of their glands for digesting insects, and the absorption of the digested matter. In a series of exuberant experiments, he tested the plants by feeding them a morsel of practically every substance he could find. Here is a partial list of them:

saliva	drops of milk	hardboiled eggs	raw meat
cheese cubes	dead flies	paper chips	wood

dried moss	caraway oil	cinders	glass
cotton-wool	cobra venom	human urine	gold-leaf
pen quill	ground peas	ground cabbage	atropine
belladonna	strychnine	quinine	curare
nicotine	adder venom	oil of cloves	water
alcohol	nitric ether	carbolic acid	stone

He was astounded at what tiny amounts of nitrogen would stimulate the leaves to action.

Experiments on carnivority were assigned to Darwin's son Frank, who grew two groups of plants. One he fed insects; the other had to take its sole sustenance from the soil. As they suspected, the insect-fed plants were more vigorous and produced more flowers and seeds. "The results," Frank concluded, "show clearly enough that insectivorous plants derive great advantage from animal food"—a finding confirmed many times since.

Carnivority in plants is now recognized in 8 families, 15 genera, and roughly 500 species, or about 0.2 percent of all flowering plants. Thus, it is a very rare occurrence. Scientists do not understand why this is so but there certainly is a correlation with habitat. In all cases, insect-eating plants are found in moist, nutrient-poor, usually acidic soils, often in sunny locations.

At the age of 72, a year before his death, Darwin published his last book, *On the Formation of Vegetable Mould by Earthworms* (1881), a simple farewell treatise, researched in his own backyard.

Today we take for granted the industriousness of worms and their important place in the ecology. In Darwin's day, all this had still to be proved, and people were startled when he claimed for worms an important part in world history. "In many parts of England," he wrote in *Earthworms,* "a weight of more than ten tons of dry earth annually passes through their bodies and is brought to the surface on each acre of land; so that the whole superficial bed of vegetable mould [topsoil] passes through their bodies in the course of every few years." One critic indignantly rejected Darwin's conclusion. "Considering their weakness and size," he wrote, "the work that they are represented to have accomplished is stupendous."

PUNCH'S FANCY PORTRAITS.—No. 54.

CHARLES ROBERT DARWIN, LL.D., F.R.S.

IN HIS *DESCENT OF MAN* HE BROUGHT HIS OWN SPECIES DOWN AS LOW AS POSSIBLE—*I.E.*, TO "A HAIRY QUADRUPED FURNISHED WITH A TAIL AND POINTED EARS, AND PROBABLY *ARBOREAL* IN ITS HABITS"—WHICH IS A REASON FOR THE VERY GENERAL INTEREST IN A "FAMILY TREE." HE HAS LATELY BEEN TURNING HIS ATTENTION TO THE "POLITIC WORM."

Caricature of Darwin and his earthworms that appeared in *Punch* magazine in 1881, the year before his death. His last book, about worms, stressed a major theme of his life's work—that small causes can produce major effects. (Author's collection)

To Darwin, it was exactly that kind of "stupendous" accomplishment through the small but steady work of natural forces that was so wonderful, which is why he chose to work on worms late in life. The progress of science has often been retarded, he wrote, by "the inability to sum up the effects of a continually recurrent cause . . . as formerly in the case of geology, and more recently in that of the principle of evolution."

Worms had originally been brought to Darwin's attention by his uncle Josiah Wedgwood, the same benefactor who had convinced Darwin's skeptical father to let him go on the *Beagle* voyage. Thirty years before, Darwin had noticed that stones scattered in fields tended to sink and become buried with time, and Wedgwood suggested that they were being covered by worm castings.

Darwin then began adding observations from other fields near his home. One had been plowed in 1841 and was called by his sons "the stony field," as it was thickly covered with small and large flints. In the *Earthworms* book, Darwin noted:

> When [my sons] ran down the slope the stones clattered together. I remember doubting whether I should live to see these larger flints covered with vegetable mould and turf . . . [but] after thirty years (1871) a horse could gallop over the compact turf . . . and not strike a single stone . . . The transformation was wonderful [and was] certainly the work of the worms.

Once Darwin got hold of a subject, he pursued it for all it was worth. He had his son Horace design a round, heavy stone, known as the "wormstone," which had a gauge in its center. Placed in his garden, the device was supposed to measure the rate at which the stone sank into the earth. One of Horace's wormstones, still kept mostly above ground, can be seen in the garden at Down House today.

In 1877, Darwin even took the long rail journey to Stonehenge to observe how far worms might have buried the ancient "Druidical stones." His sons helped dig test holes near the monolith's bases, and Darwin duly recorded that the great stones had hardly penetrated the earth, showing a lack of industriousness by Stonehenge's worms. In his search for nature's truths, Darwin literally left no stone unturned. He brought pots full of worms into the house to measure their activity at various temperatures and even had Frank play notes on the bassoon and the piano to them in the drawing room to see whether they reacted to higher or lower pitched notes. (How Emma reacted to worms on her piano is not recorded.)

Returning to earthworms in his last years, Darwin was reprising one of the great themes of his life's work. In the last paragraph of the worm book, Darwin refers to another animal of "lowly organization," the coral. In his very first scientific theory, published in *On the Formation of Coral Reefs* (1842), he discussed how the great reefs were formed by millions of tiny creatures building higher in response to subsiding ocean floors. "Clever old man," wrote paleontologist Stephen Jay Gould a century later, "he knew full well. In his last works, he looked back to his beginning, compared those worms with his first corals, and completed his life's work in both the large and the small."

During his decline from cardiac disease in 1881, Darwin told his family he was "not the least afraid to die," and expected to be buried in the old churchyard at Downe Village. When he died on April 19, 1882, however, his powerful scientific friends petitioned for burial in Westminster Abbey, England's shrine of highest honor. Darwin's pallbearers included his old friends Huxley, Hooker, Wallace, and Lubbock, and the presidents of the Royal and Linnaean Societies, the two most prestigious scientific organizations in Britain. His final resting place is a few paces away from that of Sir Isaac Newton, another scientific immortal.

Eulogizing his old friend, Thomas Henry Huxley praised Darwin's lifelong restraint and diplomacy: "He delivered a thought-reversing doctrine to mankind with as little disturbance as possible to the deeply-rooted sentiments of the age." Yet Huxley well appreciated that, notwithstanding Darwin's gentility and conventional life-style, he had managed to reshape and revolutionize Western thought:

> *None have fought better, and none have been more fortunate than Charles Darwin. He found a great truth, trodden underfoot, reviled by bigots, and ridiculed by all the world; he lived long enough to see it, chiefly by his own efforts, irrefragably established in science, inseparably incorporated with the common thoughts of men . . . What shall a man desire more than this?*

CHAPTER 11 NOTES

p. 123 "It is interesting . . ." *Origin*, p. 484.

p. 124 "the inhabitants of South America," *Origin*, p. 25.

p. 124 "During the summer of . . ." *Insectivorous Plants*, p. 1.

p. 124 "Depend on it . . ." CD to Asa Gray, c. 1863, *Life and Letters*, ii, p. 494.

p. 124 "He is treating *Drosera* . . ." Emma Darwin to Lady Lyell, August, 1860. Cited in Allen, *Darwin and His Flowers*, p. 194.

p. 125 "By Jove, I sometimes . . ." CD to Joseph D. Hooker, December 4, 1860. *More Letters*, ii, p. 267.

p. 126 "The results show clearly . . ." *Insectivorous Plants*, p. 355.

p. 126 "In many parts of England . . ." *Earthworms*, p. 280.

p. 126 "Considering their weakness . . ." *Earthworms*, p. 5.

p. 128 "the inability to sum up . . ." *Earthworms*, p. 75.

p. 128 "When [my sons] ran down . . ." *Earthworms*, p. 133.

p. 129 "Clever old man . . ." Stephen J. Gould, *Hen's Teeth and Horse's Toes* (Norton, 1983), p. 132.

p. 129 "not the least . . ." *CD Life and Letters*, iii, p. 358.

p. 129 "None have fought better . . ." T.H. Huxley, *Darwiniana*, p. 247.

12

EPILOGUE: THE SURVIVAL OF CHARLES DARWIN

"Nothing in biology makes sense," wrote geneticist Theodosius Dobzhansky, "except in the light of evolution." Every branch of the life sciences, from biochemistry to botany, has an evolutionary underpinning. Practical applications are so ubiquitous that we hardly notice the common yoke that binds them together: DNA "fingerprinting" in the courtroom, bioengineering of livestock and plants in agriculture, medical strategies to combat resistant strains of bacteria, conservation programs for endangered species, growing awareness of plantetary ecology. All are joined together by a basic, shared assumption—the idea of evolution, which only 150 years ago was considered unscientific and downright immoral.

An impolite and unruly idea that simply refuses to stay put, the theory of evolution by natural selection long ago leaped the boundaries of biology to influence an astounding variety of fields: science fiction novels, children's toys, Hollywood movies, even religious and political movements, philosophy, and law.

Darwin and his friends were well aware that they were making history and breaking new ground using very fragmentary evidence. They would have enjoyed recent developments in evolutionary biology: molecular clocks; biochemical comparisons between species DNA; radioactive dating of rocks; the African hominid fossils; field observers living peaceably and intimately among free-living chimpanzees and gorillas.

But while we have answered many of their questions, we have also deepened the mysteries. No longer do we wonder, as Darwin did, whether paleontologists will discover a single "missing link";

we've got almost more "early man" fossils than we know what to do with. The question now is, where do they fit in the increasingly complicated picture of hominid radiation? We no longer wonder whether the abrupt gaps in the fossil record are the result of "imperfect preservation," as Darwin supposed; now we believe that they reflect great and sweeping mass extinctions—but despite promising research directions, we still don't really know why they occurred. (Many scientists believe we are in the middle of a mass extinction now, losing species at the rate of three a day.)

Romantic, wintery portrait, taken in 1878, shows Darwin near the end of his life, in black cape and country parson's hat, standing on the veranda of his home. (Courtesy American Museum of Natural History)

Scientists no longer grope, as Darwin did, for the mechanisms of inheritance. In 1865, the abbot Gregor Mendel founded the science of genetics in a monastery garden—but his ideas did not begin to flourish until 30 years after his death. At the turn of the century, "Darwinism" and "Mendelism" seemed to be incompatible to some scientists, but eventually proved to be complementary pillars of the modern life sciences. Today, biologists can construct gene maps, photograph the shape of DNA, and even "engineer" new life forms by splicing genes. But still they puzzle over just what it is that is naturally selected in normal evolution. How "random" are mutations, and what are the relative importance of adaptation and dumb luck? (During conditions of global mass extinctions, for instance, a lot of extremely well-adapted forms get wiped out.)

Darwin was first among modern scientists to insist that uncertainty is an acceptable (even inevitable) part of knowledge. Does that mean evolutionary theory is worthless, as some religionists have argued, since truths must be eternal? Thomas Huxley once asked his listeners to imagine they were lost in the countryside on a dark night, with no knowledge of the road. If someone came along and offered a flickering lantern, would you refuse it because it was only an imperfect and unsteady light? "I think not," Huxley answered himself, "I think not." Huxley believed it was a high compliment to a scientist if his work "became part of the rubble" upon which the knowledge of the next generation was erected.

Each year brings exciting new discoveries about evolution: new hominid fossils; more geophysical clues to the reasons for mass extinctions; deeper understanding of how the biosphere works; insights into the neural network of the human brain, the miniature universe of living cells. But the old questions continue to beckon us, questions that go far beyond science to the heart of philosophy, art, and religion. Artist Paul Gauguin scrawled them onto his final masterpiece: *"What are we? Where do we come from? Where will we go?"*

GLOSSARY

adaptation: Evolutionary adjustment of an organism's behavior, anatomy, or physiology to its environmental niche, including specializations for feeding, protection from weather, and reproduction.

artificial selection: Creation of new varieties of animals and plants by farmers and stockbreeders, who choose desirable ancestors and eliminate unwanted offspring for many generations.

catastrophism: Belief prevalent in the seventeenth and eighteenth centuries that geological features of the Earth were caused by supernatural forces that scooped out oceans or carved mountains in cataclysmic bursts of activity by a divine Creator.

Cirripedia: (Latin for "curl footed.") Barnacles, the diverse group of invertebrate marine organisms often found anchored to whales, ships, and dock pilings. Darwin devoted eight years to their study.

coevolution: When two or more organisms have had a profound influence on each other's evolution, as between certain flowers and hummingbirds, or ant-acacia trees and the ant colonies that inhabit them.

creationism: Belief in a literal interpretation of the Book of Genesis, especially in the idea that all species of plants and animals (including humans) were created by God as fixed "types" instantaneously and on the same day.

DNA (deoxyribonucleic acid): An organic molecule comprising two strands of nucleotides wound around each other in a double helix. It carries the genetic blueprint for all organisms except RNA viruses. DNA "fingerprinting," now widely used in the law courts, is a means of positively identifying individuals from tiny samples of skin or hair, because no two people have identical DNA.

divergence: The principle, independently discovered by both Darwin and Wallace, that species occupying the same area under conditions of intense competition tend to evolve into

135

many new species, each exploiting different niches within a similar environment.

Drosera: A group of insect-eating plants, particularly the sundew, whose behavior was first studied by Darwin. They often live in nutrient-poor bogs and obtain nitrogen by trapping and digesting insects.

ecology: The study of the interrelationships between an organism and its internal and external environment. The term, coined by Darwinian zoologist Ernst Haeckel, refers to an animal's niche or "home" (*oikos*) in nature. Often inaccurately used to refer to the politics of conservation.

evolution: Genetic change of living populations through time; descent with modification from common ancestors. Evolution does not proceed in straight lines, does not head for a final goal, and is not an inevitable progress from lower to higher forms. It works through natural selection and such other mechanisms as genetic drift and hybridization; sometimes chance plays an important role.

extinction: Termination of an evolutionary lineage; death of breeding populations, leaving no descendants.

fitness: Success of an organism in leaving descendants that resemble itself. May refer to "survival fitness" (protective colors, strength, intelligence, ability to find food) or to "reproductive fitness" (egg clutch size, ability to find many mates, etc.). Fitness is always relative to environment; in some situations, otherwise "fit" groups of animals (e.g. dinosaurs) may be swept away by changing conditions.

gauchos: Argentinian cowboys; Darwin rode horseback with these rough, independent cattle herders of the pampas, or plains.

gene: The biochemical unit or segment of DNA by which an organism's characteristics and developmental program are physically transmitted from generation to generation.

gene pool: The sum total of genes within a breeding population or species.

gradualism: Darwin's belief that evolution proceeds by "slow, insensible degrees" at a more or less steady rate over vast periods of time—a notion that is not supported by present knowledge of the fossil record. It remains true, however, in the sense that evolution proceeds by the gradual modification of populations, rather than by the sudden origin of new types.

hominid: "Near-humans," members of the family Hominidae, a primate group that includes australopithecines, apes, and humans.

hybrid: The offspring of crosses between varieties or species.

keystone species: A species that is crucial to an ecosystem, sometimes even creating or modifying an environment, enabling other species to find niches. Examples: coral polyps that build reef habitats, elephants that level scrub forests and dig waterholes, beavers that create ponds by damming streams.

longitudes: Measurements or lines through the Earth's poles that divide the planet into segments, like a sliced orange, as an aid to accurate navigation.

materialism: Scientific assumption that seeks causes in the natural properties of matter, leaving gods, ghosts, or spirits out of the theorizing.

morphology: Study of the form of animals, including their bones, organs, muscles, and other structures.

natural history: Nineteenth-century name for the study of nature by someone of wide general knowledge; includes what later became such specialties as zoology, biology, geology, botany, animal behavior, ecology, etc.

natural selection: The major mechanism by which species populations change or evolve over time. Overproduction of eggs, seeds, or offspring means that only a small percentage will survive to reproduce the species. Selection acts upon the natural variation among these individuals; those with any slight heritable advantage in a given environment will contribute more of their genes to the next generation.

naturalist: One who studies natural history, possessing a knowledge of botany, geology, zoology, what later became known as biology, and sometimes even anthropology (originally the study of tribal peoples.) Today "naturalist" is applied mainly to field researchers who observe animals in their natural habitats. Those who try to save both from destruction are called conservation biologists.

phrenology: See physiognomy.

physiognomy: A pseudo-scienctific fad of the nineteenth century that involved "reading" a person's character from his or her facial features. Allied to phrenology, a similar belief that the bumps on people's skulls can reveal their abilities and personality traits.

population: A community of potentially interbreeding individuals, usually sharing a particular geographic area.

punctuationalism: Theory that species populations remain stable, changing little over vast periods of time, punctuated by episodes of rapid evolution, after which the new species become stable again. ("Rapid" in this sense can still mean hundreds of thousands of years.) Advanced by Eldredge and Gould in the 1970s to account for the episodic nature of the fossil record.

saltation: The idea, disavowed by Darwin, that new species originate by sudden change ("leaps") in one or a few individual organisms, which become the progenitors of new species.

sexual selection: An evolutionary mechanism proposed by Darwin to account for such phenomena as the peacock's tail or the stag's antlers. Such complex structures appear to have evolved to increase attractiveness to members of the opposite sex or to compete with sexual rivals.

sociobiology: Study of the biological and evolutionary basis of social behavior in animals, including humans.

Spiritualism: A belief, common in many times and places, in a disembodied spirit or consciousness separate from a material body, including the notion that the living can communicate with the dead. Spiritualism was particularly popular in nineteenth-century England and America, and enlisted believers even among the scientific community (e.g., Alfred Russel Wallace).

symbiosis: Mutualism among organisms, whereby animals or plants trade resources. Examples are the clown barb fish and the sea anemone, or humans and dairy cows.

uniformitarianism: Charles Lyell's principle that major geologic features of the Earth can be explained by small, ordinary forces (e.g., erosion by water or wind, volcanic activity) acting slowly and gradually over immense periods of time. These forces are, for the most part, no different than those that can still be observed at work on the Earth today.

FURTHER READING

Books by Charles Darwin:

Although original publication dates are given below, most of Darwin's works can be obtained in recent reprint, facsimile, and paperback editions.

Journal (also known as *Voyage of the Beagle*). London: 1839. Published in several versions. Darwin's exciting chronicle of travel, adventure, and the romance of natural history. A bestseller in its time, it has remained in print for more than 150 years. Annotated reprint, New York: Anchor Books, 1962.

Structure and Distribution of Coral Reefs. London: 1842. Darwin's first scientific book; its basic theory still stands.

On the Origin of Species by Means of Natural Selection. London: John Murray, 1859. Difficult reading, but a masterpiece of science. The book that founded evolutionary biology.

The Various Contrivances by Which Orchids are Fertilised by Insects. London: Murray, 1862. A technical book, applying evolutionary theory to cases of plant-insect coevolution.

Descent of Man. London: John Murray, 1871. On human evolution and sexual selection.

Expression of the Emotions in Man and Animals. London: Murray, 1872. The pioneering work on the evolution of behavior.

Earthworms and Vegetable Mould. Darwin's last book, about the immense power of small steady forces over time.

Darwin, Charles. *Autobiography* (Nora Barlow, ed.) New York: Norton, 1958. Darwin's own brief account of his life, with cuts made in previous editions restored.

About Charles Darwin:

Allan, Mea. *Darwin and His Flowers.* New York: Taplinger, 1977. A highly readable roundup of Darwin's contributions to botany.

Brent, Peter. *Charles Darwin; A Man of Enlarged Curiosity.* New York: Harper and Row, 1981. A solid, enjoyable, detailed biography.

Clark, Ronald. *The Survival of Charles Darwin.* New York: Random House, 1984. Readable account of Darwin's life, combined with history of his scientific legacy to the present.

Colp, Ralph. *To Be an Invalid; the Illness of Charles Darwin.* Chicago: University of Chicago, 1977. An erudite psychiatrist's view of Darwin's medical problems.

Gould, Stephen Jay. *Ever Since Darwin.* New York: Norton, 1979. Engrossing essays, ranging from evolutionary theory to insights into Darwin's character.

Hyman, Stanley. *The Tangled Bank; Darwin, Marx, Frazer and Freud as Imaginative Writers.* New York: Atheneum, 1962. Explores literary and rhetorical aspects of Darwin's writing style.

Irvine, William. *Apes, Angels, and Victorians; The Story of Darwin, Huxley and Evolution.* London: Weidenfeld & Nicolson, 1956. First-rate history of two great men and their battle to revolutionize biology.

Moore, James, and Adrian Desmond. *Darwin.* New York: Warner Books: 1992. A meticulous biography with special emphasis on the political and religious climate of Darwin's century.

About the Idea of Evolution:

Appleman, Philip, ed. *Darwin; a Norton Critical Edition.* New York: W. W. Norton, 1970. A solid, wide-ranging anthology of source materials.

Barber, Lynn. *The Heyday of Natural History.* Garden City: Doubleday, 1980. Excellent, entertaining overview of Darwin's place in the history of natural history.

Bowler, Peter J. *Evolution: the History of an Idea.* Berkeley: University of California Press, 1984. College-course level intellectual history. Textbook-like but authoritative.

Cronin, Helene. *The Ant and the Peacock: Altruism and Sexual Selection from Darwin to Today.* Cambridge, England: Cambridge University Press, 1991.

Eiseley, Loren. *Darwin's Century; Evolution and the Men Who Discovered It.* New York: Doubleday, 1958. A perennial on college campuses by one of the best writers on evolution and the history of ideas.

Futuyma, Douglas. *Science on Trial; the Case for Evolution.* New York: Pantheon, 1982.

Gould, Stephen Jay. *The Panda's Thumb.* New York: Norton, 1980. Literate, entertaining essays on Darwin's life and thought, as well as insights into natural history by America's "evolutionist laureate."

———, ed. *The Book of Life: An Illustrated History of the Evolution of Life on Earth.* New York: W.W. Norton, 1993. An authoritative, lavishly illustrated roundup of our current knowledge of evolution by top experts, written in clear, nontechnical English.

Greene, John C. *The Death of Adam; Evolution and its Impact on Western Thought.* Ames: Iowa State University Press, 1959. An excellent intellectual history, including such juicy tidbits as the paleontological contributions of President Thomas Jefferson.

Hitching, Francis. *The Neck of the Giraffe; Where Darwin Went Wrong.* New Haven: Ticknor & Fields, 1982. Current debates and controversies in evolutionary theory for the general reader.

Kitcher, Philip. *Abusing Science; the Case Against Creationism.* Cambridge: MIT, 1982. A worthwhile collection of articles on the never-ending controversy.

Kohn, David, editor. *The Darwinian Heritage.* Princeton: Princeton University Press, 1985. Heavy going, imposing roundup of current topics in Darwinian scholarship.

Mayr, Ernst. *The Growth of Biological Thought; Diversity, Evolution and Inheritance.* Cambridge: Harvard University Press, 1982. A definitive work for thoroughgoing, advanced students of biological history.

Milner, Richard B. *The Encyclopedia of Evolution; Humanity's Search for Its Origins.* New York: Facts On File, 1990 (paperback: Henry Holt & Co., 1993). Hundreds of essays on the history of evolutionary ideas in biology, philosophy, art, law, and popular culture, with brief biographies of scientists.

Reader, John. *Missing Links; the Hunt for Earliest Man.* London: Collins, 1981.

———. *The Rise of Life.* New York: Knopf, 1988. Reader's books are clear, nontechnical presentations of the current view of the evolution of life and the search for remains of early humans.

About the *Beagle* Voyage:

FitzRoy, Capt. Robert. *Narrative of the Surveying Voyages of His Majesty's Ships Adventure, & the Beagle.* London: 1839. The captain's account supplements Darwin's observations.

Keynes, R. D., ed. *Charles Darwin's Beagle Diary.* Cambridge: Cambridge University Press, 1979. Useful compilation of *Beagle* material from Darwin, FitzRoy, others, with paintings by *Beagle* artists.

Marks, Richard L. *Three Men of the Beagle.* New York: Alfred A. Knopf, 1991. A novelist's account of the intertwined adventures of Darwin, FitzRoy, and Jemmy Button.

Mellersh, H. E. L. *Fitzroy of the Beagle.* London: Mason and Lipscomb, 1968. Most complete, well-written biography of Darwin's captain.

Moorehead, Alan. *Darwin and the Beagle.* New York: Harper and Row, 1969. Superb, dramatic, well-illustrated account of the voyage.

Steadman, David, and Zousmer, Steven. *Galapagos; Discovery on Darwin's Island.* Washington, D.C.: Smithsonian, 1988. Brings discoveries about Galapagos wildlife up to date.

Books by and about Alfred Russel Wallace:

Brackman, Arnold C. *A Delicate Arrangement; the Strange Case of Charles Darwin and Alfred Russel Wallace.* New York: Times Books, 1980. A journalist's study of history's relative treatment of Darwin and Wallace, giving Wallace his due at last— but marred by shrill tone and sloppy scholarship.

Brooks, John. *Just Before the Origin; Alfred Russel Wallace's Theory of Evolution.* New York: Columbia University Press, 1983. Solid, scholarly assessment of Wallace's contribution.

Marchant, James, ed. *Alfred Russel Wallace; Letters and Reminiscenses.* New York: Harper, 1914. Contains the Darwin-Wallace correspondence and much else of interest.

McKinney, H. Lewis. *Wallace and Natural Selection.* New Haven: Yale University Press, 1972. An ingenious investigation into what Darwin knew about Wallace's theory, and when he knew it.

Smith, Charles H., ed. *Alfred Russel Wallace: an Anthology of His Shorter Writings.* New York: Oxford University Press, 1991. A goldmine for Wallace scholars.

Wallace, Alfred Russel. *Travels on the Amazon and Rio Negro.* London: Ward Lock, 1903. One of the great books of natural history and travel; as entertaining and remarkable as Darwin's *Voyage of the Beagle.*

———. *The Malay Archipelago.* New York: Macmillan, 1872.

———. *My Life.* New York: Dodd, Mead, 1905. If your library has this rare book, read Wallace's story in his own words.

———. *The Wonderful Century.* New York: Dodd, Mead, 1904. Wallace looks back on the scientific accomplishments of the 19th century, from a perspective just inside the twentieth.

———. *Social Environment and Moral Progress.* New York: Funk and Wagnalls, 1913. Wallace's last book: a plea for curbs on exploitative robber barons, and advocating wilderness conservation, pacifism, women's rights, and antivaccination.

Primary Sources:

Barlow, Nora. *Darwin and Henslow; the History of an Idea.* Annotated correspondence between young Darwin and his Cambridge mentor.

Barrett, Paul H. *The Collected Papers of Charles Darwin.* Chicago: University of Chicago Press, 1977. Darwin's scientific articles and reviews.

——— et al. *Charles Darwin's Notebooks 1836–1844.* Ithaca, New York: Cornell University Press, 1987.n.

Burkhardt, Frederick and Sydney Smith, et al. *Collected Correspondence of Charles Darwin.* Cambridge: Cambridge University Press, 1985 et seq. (Seven volumes published as of 1992). The definitive, ongoing, multimillion-dollar project to publish all of Darwin's correspondence—almost 20,000 letters.

Darwin, Charles. *Diary of the Beagle.* An early account of the *Beagle* voyage that differs in some interesting respects from the *Journal of Researches* or *Voyage of the Beagle,* published later.

Darwin, Francis, ed. *Life and Letters of Charles Darwin.* New York: Appleton, 1906. Still-useful selection of letters and personal insights by Darwin's son.

Huxley, Leonard, ed. *Life and Letters of Thomas Henry Huxley.* London: Macmillan, 1900. Rich source of material by and about "Darwin's bulldog," the zoologist, essayist, and educator who claimed he ate bishops for breakfast.

Huxley, Thomas Henry. *Collected Essays.* London: Macmillan 1885–1890.

Also of Interest:

Bates, Henry W. *Naturalist on the River Amazons.* 1863. Reprint, London: Viking-Penguin, 1989. A natural history classic by Wallace's partner in early explorations, still in print.

Bibby, Cyril, ed. *The Essence of T. H. Huxley.* New York: Macmillan, 1967. Wide-ranging collection of Huxley quotes from the lectures, essays, and letters.

Clark, Ronald. *The Huxleys.* New York: McGraw-Hill, 1968. Thomas Henry Huxley founded an intellectual and literary lineage that included his grandsons Julian, the biologist, and Aldous, the novelist. This is the story of a remarkable and accomplished family.

Dupree, A. Hunter. *Asa Gray: American Botanist, Friend of Darwin* Baltimore: Johns Hopkins, 1988. Solid biography of Darwin's botanical disciple in America, who tried to combine theology and evolution.

King-Hele, Desmond. *Erasmus Darwin; Grandfather of Charles Darwin.* New York: Scribners, 1963. Demonstrates how Charles Darwin's gifted grandfather began the evolutionary inquiry that became a family enterprise.

Milner, Richard B. "Darwin for the Prosecution, Wallace for the Defense: Part I. How Two Great Naturalists Put the Supernatural on Trial." *North Country Naturalist,* 2 (1990), 19–35.

———. "Darwin for the Prosecution, Wallace for the Defense: Part II. Spirit of a Dead Controversy." *North Country Naturalist,* 2 (1990), 37–49. The author's original research, giving the basis for the "Ghostbusters" chapter in this book.

Raverat, Gwen. *Period Piece; a Cambridge Childhood.* London: Faber & Faber, 1952. Charming reminiscences by Darwin's granddaughter.

Stocking, George. *Victorian Anthropology.* New York: The Free Press, Macmillan, 1987. With fascinating (though often technical) detail, a historian of science chronicles the Victorian social context in which anthropological studies originated.

INDEX

Illustrations are indicated by *italic* numbers.
Glossary items are marked with a "*g*".